AVENUES
English Skills

2

Lynne Gaetz

PEARSON

Montréal

Managing Editor
Sharnee Chait

Editor
Lucie Turcotte

Copy Editor
Mairi MacKinnon

Proofreader
Katie Moore

Coordinator, Rights and Permissions
Pierre-Richard Bernier

Photo Research and Permissions
Marie-Chantal Masson

Art Director
Hélène Cousineau

Graphic Design Coordinator
Lyse LeBlanc

Book and Cover Design
Frédérique Bouvier

Book Layout
Interscript

Illustrations
p. 13, Martin Tremblay
p. 111, Louise Catherine Bergeron

Cover Artwork
Pietro Adamo. *Citta Series*, 2009. Mixed media on canvas, 40 x 40 inches. Courtesy of Progressive Fine Art and Galerie Beauchamp. © 2011 Artist Pietro Adamo.

© ÉDITIONS DU RENOUVEAU PÉDAGOGIQUE INC. (ERPI), 2012
ERPI publishes and distributes PEARSON ELT products in Canada.

5757, Cypihot Street
Saint-Laurent, Québec H4S 1R3
CANADA
Telephone: 1 800 263-3678
Fax: 1 866 334-0448
infoesl@pearsonerpi.com
http://pearsonelt.ca

All rights reserved.
No part of this publication may be reproduced, stored in a retrieval system, or transmitted in any form or by any means, electronic, mechanical, photocopying, recording, or otherwise without the prior written permission of ÉDITIONS DU RENOUVEAU PÉDAGOGIQUE INC.

Registration of copyright – Bibliothèque et Archives nationales du Québec, 2012
Registration of copyright – Library and Archives Canada, 2012

Printed in Canada   23456789   SO 16 15 14 13
ISBN 978-2-7613-4458-6   134458 ABCD   ENV94

Acknowledgements
I would like to express sincere thanks to
- Lucie Turcotte for her dedicated editing and her magnificent job of polishing this book;
- Sharnee Chait for her valuable expertise;
- Julie Hough for her enthusiastic words that helped ignite this project;
- Frédérique Bouvier and Interscript for the creative layout;
- Mairi MacKinnon and Katie Moore for their careful work on the manuscript and proofs;
- My students at Collège Lionel-Groulx for their insightful feedback;
- Diego Pelaez for his valuable contributions to the manuscript and the Companion Website;
- Rebeka Pelaez for her optimistic attitude as she worked on the transcripts and tests;
- The teachers who kindly provided feedback.

Credits

Chapter 1, pp. 4–5 "Why I Travel" by Ben Casnocha reprinted with the permission of the author. p. 7 Audio text "Out-of-Control Travel Adventure" © Canadian Broadcasting Corporation. pp. 9–10 "Cultural Minefields" by William Ecenbarger © 2008, Los Angeles Times; reprinted with permission. p. 12 Video segment "Ocean Survival – Part One: Rip Currents" © ABC News. p. 13 Video segment "Ocean Survival – Part Two: Tsunami" © ABC News. pp. 14–16 "Record-Breaking Travel Adventure" reprinted with the permission of Graham Hughes.

Chapter 2, p. 23 Audio text "Awesome Things" © Canadian Broadcasting Corporation. pp. 25–26 "The Botched Tan" by Sarah Stanfield reprinted with permission. This article first appeared in Salon.com, at http://www.Salon.com; an online version remains in the Salon archives. pp. 28–29 "Winter Love" by Josh Freed reprinted with the permission of the author. pp. 32–33 "Act Happy" by Albert Nerenberg reprinted with the permission of the author. p. 35 Video segment "Living in Denmark" © ABC News.

Chapter 3, p. 42 Audio text "Lady Gaga: Poser or Pioneer?" © Canadian Broadcasting Corporation. pp. 43–44 "Interview with Melissa Auf der Maur" reprinted with the permission of Melissa Auf der Maur. pp. 46–47 "Interview with Jay Baruchel" by Jasper Anson reprinted with permission; Copyright © 2010 AskMen.com Solutions Inc. All rights reserved. p. 50 Video segment "TV, Afghanistan Style" © Canadian Broadcasting Corporation. pp. 52–53 "Art and Plagiarism: Does Originality Matter?" by Laura Miller reprinted with permission. This article first appeared in Salon.com, at http://www.Salon.com; an online version remains in the Salon archives.

Chapter 4, p. 63 Video segment "Damn Heels" © Canadian Broadcasting Corporation. pp. 65–66 "The Allure of Apple" by Juan Rodriguez reprinted with the express permission of Montreal Gazette Group Inc., a Postmedia Network Partnership. p. 68 Audio text "Generic Brands" © Age of Persuasion; courtesy of Terry O'Reilly.

Chapter 5, pp. 75–77 "My Personal History of E-Addiction" by Steve Almond reprinted with permission. This article first appeared in Salon.com, at http://www.Salon.com; an online version remains in the Salon archives. p. 79 Video segment "Interview with Mark Zuckerberg" © BBC Motion Gallery. p. 85 Audio text "The Peep Diaries" © Canadian Broadcasting Corporation. pp. 86–88 "Gone with the Windows" by Dorothy Nixon reprinted with the permission of the author.

Chapter 6, p. 98 Video segment "The End of Suburbia" (excerpt) © The End of Suburbia Inc. pp. 99–101 "The Utopian Town of Celebration" by Douglas Frantz and Catherine Collins reprinted with permission.
pp. 105–106 "Chaos in the Streets" by Linda Baker reprinted with permission. This article first appeared in Salon.com, at http://www.Salon.com; an online version remains in the Salon archives.

Chapter 7, pp. 113–115 "Flash Mobs, Flash Robs, and Riots" by Diego Pelaez reprinted with the permission of the author. p. 118 Audio text "Public Shaming" © Canadian Broadcasting Corporation. p. 126 Video segment "Ask Me Anything: I'm Homeless" © Canadian Broadcasting Corporation.

Reading Supplement, p. 130 "Toggling the Switch" by Alicia Gifford reprinted with the permission of the author.

This book is printed on paper made in Québec from 100% post-consumer recycled materials, processed chlorine-free, certified Eco-Logo, and manufactured using biogas energy.

Preface

Avenues 2: English Skills is the second of a three-level series. Designed for intermediate students of English as a second language, *Avenues 2* is a comprehensive integrated skills text. As the author of the *Brass Tacks*, *Brass Ring*, and *Open* series, I have spent many years exploring what works in my classroom and developing material that will engage and inform students.

In *Avenues 2: English Skills*, seven chapters focus on contemporary themes that will interest and challenge students. The Start-Up activity in each chapter introduces students to the chapter's theme. Vocabulary Boosts and online exercises help students develop a more varied vocabulary. Blog posts, excerpts from books and textbooks, magazine and newspaper articles, as well as short stories, expose students to a variety of ideas and writing styles. In the Take Action! section near the end of each chapter, there are additional writing and speaking prompts. Chapters end with revising and editing exercises that can help students improve their writing skills. At the end of the book, four writing workshops contain detailed information about the paragraph and essay and revising techniques.

Because question forms are difficult for students to master, most chapters contain question activities. Additionally, visual aids help students retain concepts. Scattered throughout the chapters, grammar tips remind students about key concepts.

Avenues 2: English Skills is accompanied by a learning-centred website, the *Avenues 2: English Skills Companion Website Plus*. To provide maximum flexibility for teachers, every reading, watching, and listening activity in the skills book has two sets of different questions: 1) Textbook questions can be taken up in class; 2) Online questions can be assigned as homework or done in a classroom lab. The automated grading function allows students to check their results. Using the grade tracker, you can conveniently monitor their progress and verify that homework was done. To help students do better in reading tests, including Benchmark and TESOL tests, the website also contains a Reading Strategies section filled with practice exercises.

In the Teacher Section of the Companion Website, you will find a variety of class-tested reading and listening tests. If you want to modify a particular test, simply download the Word document and make adjustments. The Teacher Section also contains evaluation grids as well as transcripts for the audio and visual material. An eText version of this book is included for projection purposes.

Avenues 2: English Skills includes more material than necessary for a course of forty-five hours, allowing you to use different chapters when you've exhausted certain topics. Additionally, you can present chapters in whatever sequence you prefer.

Complementing the themes in this book is *Avenues 2: English Grammar*. If students have particular difficulties with a grammatical concept, they can try additional online exercises created for the *Avenues 2: English Grammar Companion Website Plus*.

Finally, I'm delighted with the decision to print my books on recycled paper.

Lynne Gaetz

Highlights

Warm-up activities provide a relevant introduction to each chapter's theme.

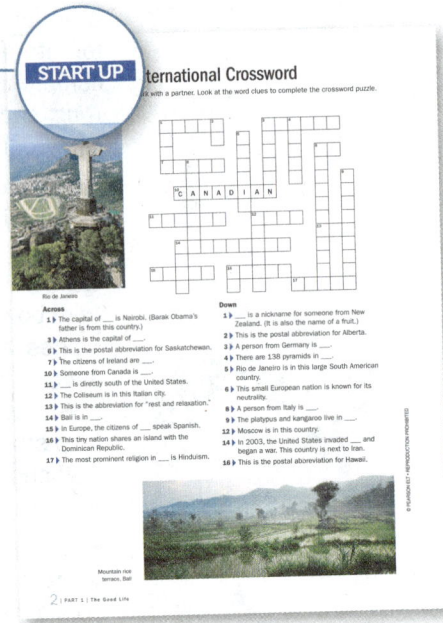

Effective strategies help students improve their reading skills. Online practice allows them to prepare for reading tests, including Benchmark and TESOL tests.

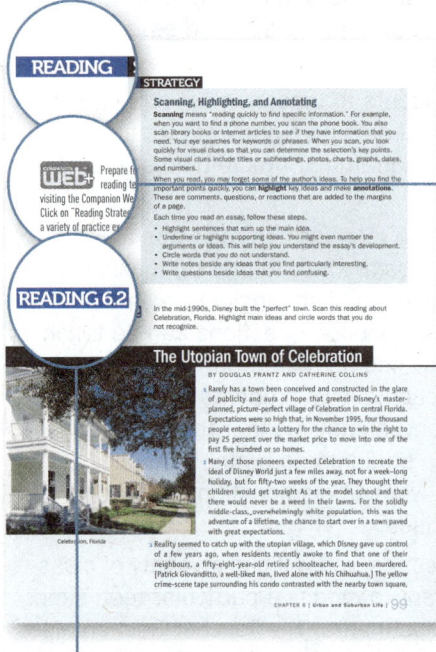

The *Avenues 2: English Skills Companion Website Plus* contains additional reading and listening material for further practice. It also includes vocabulary exercises and extra comprehension questions for all the reading and listening activities in the book.

Exercises and useful tips allow students to practise pronunciation.

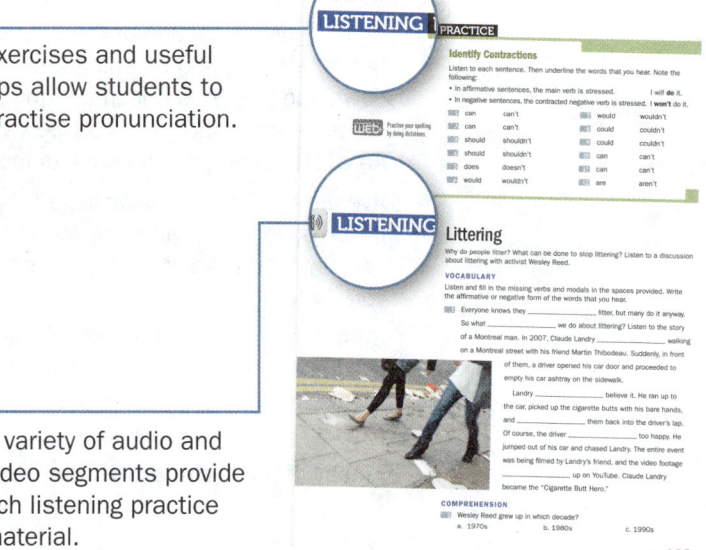

Texts taken from a variety of sources expose students to different writing styles and ideas.

A variety of audio and video segments provide rich listening practice material.

IV | AVENUES 2

Vocabulary Boosts help students to build their vocabulary, including idioms.

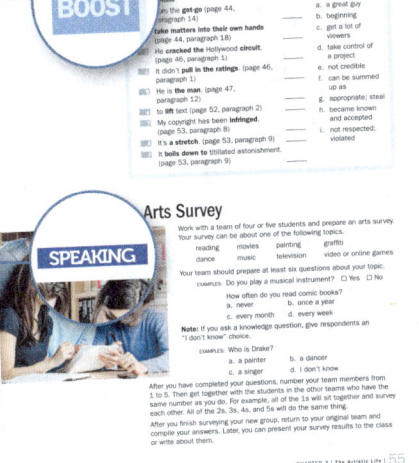

In each chapter, the Take Action! section includes additional writing and speaking topics as well as presentation tips.

Speaking activities particularly emphasize question formation.

The Revising and Editing section helps students to develop their writing skills and to prepare for writing tests, including the Benchmark and TESOL tests.

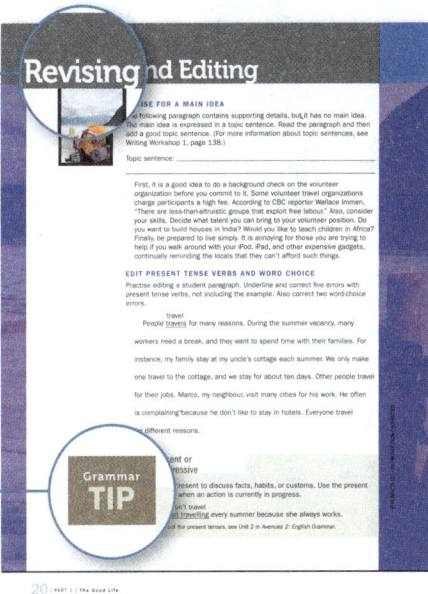

Throughout the book, Grammar Tips cover key concepts, which are further explored in *Avenues 2: English Grammar*.

- A Reading Supplement invites students to engage in a reading group activity based on a short story.
- Four Writing Workshops provide detailed explanations about the paragraph and the essay.

HIGHLIGHTS | V

Scope and Sequence

		READING	WRITING	LISTENING/WATCHING
PART 1: THE GOOD LIFE	**CHAPTER 1:** On the Road	• Use context clues • Recognize cognates • Identify main and supporting ideas • Read: a narrative blog; a newspaper article; an interview	• Write a structured paragraph • Write essays using the present and past tenses • Write topic sentences • Revise and edit paragraphs	• Listen: for third-person singular verbs; for main ideas • Listen to an interview with a traveller • Watch two videos about ocean survival
	CHAPTER 2: The Pleasure Principle	• Practise using a dictionary • Read: an online magazine article; two newspaper articles • Identify main and supporting ideas • Identify vocabulary in context	• Brainstorm ideas • Write essays that relate to the chapter's readings • Write interview questions using a variety of question words • Revise and edit paragraphs	• Identify silent letters • Listen to an interview about awesome things • Watch a video about the happiest place on earth
	CHAPTER 3: The Artistic Life	• Use critical thinking techniques • Identify main and supporting ideas • Read: two interviews; an online article • Do a pair reading	• Write an introduction • Write questions and answers • Write survey questions • Write an essay • Edit a paragraph	• Identify past tense verbs • Listen to an interview about Lady Gaga • Watch a report about television in Afghanistan
PART 2: CONSUMPTION AND TECHNOLOGY	**CHAPTER 4:** Great Ideas	• Identify the thesis and topic sentences • Identify vocabulary in context • Read: a personal essay; a newspaper article • Proofread an essay	• Write a summary • Write about a partner's responses • Write an essay about brands or consumerism • Use coordinators and subordinators • Edit paragraphs	• Listen for main ideas • Listen to details about prices and dates • Watch a video about a great product on *Dragon's Den* • Listen to a discussion about generic brands
	CHAPTER 5: The Digital Age	• Identify the thesis and topic sentences • Read: a narrative blog; an online article; a personal essay • Use critical thinking techniques • Make inferences	• Write questions and definitions • Write an argument or cause and effect essay • Use transitional expressions • Edit an essay	• Listen for main ideas and details • Watch an interview with Mark Zuckerberg • Listen to a discussion about peep culture
PART 3: URBAN ISSUES	**CHAPTER 6:** Urban and Suburban Life	• Identify the message • Read: an argument essay; a newspaper article; an online article • Identify the main idea and understand details • Use critical thinking techniques • Scan and highlight a text	• Write questions and definitions • Describe an ideal house • Write about urban and suburban living • Write a conclusion • Edit an essay	• Listen for main ideas and details • Watch a documentary about the end of suburbia • Listen to an interview about littering
	CHAPTER 7: Social Issues	• Respond to a short story • Identify main ideas and understand details • Identify short story elements • Read: an online article; a short story • Identify the message	• Write questions using a variety of tenses • Write a response to a film • Support opinions • Revise for sentence variety • Edit for mixed errors	• Listen to a police report • Identify physical description terms • Listen for word stress and sentence stress • Watch a video about a homeless man • Listen to a discussion about public shaming
	Reading Supplement	• Read a short story • Do a reading group activity		

SPEAKING/ PRONUNCIATION	VOCABULARY	GRAMMAR	REVISING AND EDITING
• Discuss body language • Share information about travel preferences • Ask and answer questions • Make an oral presentation	• Learn about country names, nationalities; verbs (gestures) • Study travel vocabulary • Identify cognates and false cognates	• Form questions • Learn capitalization rules • Use third-person singular verbs • Identify verb tense and word choice errors	• Revise a paragraph for the main idea • Edit for verb tense and word choice errors
• Discuss simple pleasures • Compare nations • Interview a partner • Ask and answer questions • Pronounce *gh* • Make an oral presentation	• Learn idioms and expressions • Read dictionary definitions • Act out verbs • Distinguish between *fun*, *funny*, *humour*, *mood*, and *moody*	• Use a variety of question words • Use present, past, and future tenses • Edit for errors with nouns and determiners	• Revise a paragraph for supporting details • Edit for nouns and determiners
• Discuss cultural icons • Compare two Canadian performers • Play "The Name Game" • Pronounce past tense verbs and sentences • Discuss plagiarism	• Describe clothing and consumer environments • Study idioms and expressions	• Recognize irregular past tense verbs • Form questions • Identify errors in past-tense verbs	• Revise for an introduction • Edit for verb tense
• Discuss past trends • Discuss novelty items • Do a "Name That Product" activity • Make an oral presentation	• Identify numbers • Define words • Use descriptive adjectives • Describe objects	• Identify numbers • Form questions • Identify possessive adjective and pronoun errors • Use adjectives	• Revise for sentence variety • Edit for pronouns and question forms
• Discuss past and present technology • Discuss addictions • Ask "Have you ever ...?" questions • Interview a partner • Discuss pros and cons • Pronounce *h*, *t*, and *th*	• Study idioms and expressions • Identify phrasal verbs • Study technical terms	• Use the present perfect tense • Form questions • Distinguish between *t* and *th* • Identify verb tense, plural, and pronoun errors	• Revise for transitional words and expressions • Edit an essay for verb tense, plural, and pronoun errors
• Discuss the ideal house • Make comparisons • Make a public service announcement • Identify negative contracted forms • Make an oral presentation	• Describe houses • Study house-related vocabulary • Distinguish between *suburb*, *suburban*, *sprawl*, etc. • Use comparative forms of adjectives	• Use modals • Form questions • Use comparative and superlative forms • Make comparisons • Identify errors in comparative forms	• Revise for a conclusion • Edit an essay for comparatives and word choice
• Discuss crime cases • Discuss flash mobs • Have a team discussion about public shaming • Come to a consensus about punishments for criminals • Make an oral presentation	• Study crime-related terms • Identify physical description vocabulary • Act out verbs	• Use different verb tenses • Ask and answer questions • Use modals • Make comparisons	• Revise for adequate support • Edit for modals

SCOPE AND SEQUENCE | VII

Table of Contents

PART 1: THE GOOD LIFE

CHAPTER 1 **On the Road** ... 1
- START UP: International Crossword ... 2
- READING 1.1: "Why I Travel" ... 4
- LISTENING PRACTICE:
  - 1. Pronounce –s on Verbs ... 6
  - 2. Pronounce Complete Sentences ... 6
- LISTENING: Out-of-Control Travel Adventure ... 7
- SPEAKING: Body Language ... 8
- READING 1.2: "Cultural Minefields" ... 9
- WATCHING: Ocean Survival ... 12
  - Part 1: Rip Currents ... 12
  - Part 2: Tsunami ... 13
- READING 1.3: "Record-Breaking Travel Adventure" ... 14
- SPEAKING: Travel Interview ... 17
- TAKE ACTION! ... 18
- REVISING AND EDITING ... 20

CHAPTER 2 **The Pleasure Principle** ... 21
- START UP: Simple Pleasures ... 22
- LISTENING PRACTICE:
  - 1. Identify Silent Letters ... 22
  - 2. Pronounce *gh* ... 23
- LISTENING: Awesome Things ... 23
- READING 2.1: "The Botched Tan" ... 25
- SPEAKING: Pleasure ... 27
- READING 2.2: "Winter Love" ... 28
- SPEAKING: Strong Emotions ... 31
- READING 2.3: "Act Happy" ... 32
- SPEAKING: The Greatest Country ... 35
- WATCHING: Living in Denmark ... 35
- TAKE ACTION! ... 36
- REVISING AND EDITING ... 38

CHAPTER 3 **The Artistic Life** ... 39
- START UP: Arts Quiz ... 40
- LISTENING PRACTICE:
  - 1. Pronounce Past Tense Verbs ... 41
  - 2. Pronounce Sentences and Identify Verbs ... 41

LISTENING: Lady Gaga: Poser or Pioneer?	42
READING 3.1: "Interview with Melissa Auf der Maur"	43
READING 3.2: "Interview with Jay Baruchel"	46
SPEAKING: The Name Game	49
WATCHING: TV, Afghanistan Style	50
READING 3.3: "Art and Plagiarism: Does Originality Matter?"	52
SPEAKING: Arts Survey	55
TAKE ACTION!	56
REVISING AND EDITING	57

PART 2: CONSUMPTION AND TECHNOLOGY

CHAPTER 4 Great Ideas — 59

START UP: What's the Trend?	60
READING 4.1: "Novelty Items"	61
WATCHING: Damn Heels	63
SPEAKING: Name That Product	65
READING 4.2: "The Allure of Apple"	65
LISTENING PRACTICE: Identify Numbers	68
LISTENING: Generic Brands	68
SPEAKING: Great Decisions	69
TAKE ACTION!	70
REVISING AND EDITING	71

CHAPTER 5 The Digital Age — 73

START UP: Tech Life	74
READING 5.1: "My Personal History of E-Addiction"	75
SPEAKING: Addictive Behaviour	78
WATCHING: Interview with Mark Zuckerberg	79
READING 5.2: "YouTube Hits"	80
SPEAKING: Have You Ever …?	83
LISTENING PRACTICE:	
1. Pronounce *h*, *t*, and *th*	84
2. Pronunciation	85
LISTENING: The Peep Diaries	85
READING 5.3: "Gone with the Windows"	86
TAKE ACTION!	90
REVISING AND EDITING	91

PART 3: URBAN ISSUES

CHAPTER 6 Urban and Suburban Life 93
- START UP: The Ideal House 94
- READING 6.1: "Architecture Matters" 95
- WATCHING: The End of Suburbia 98
- READING 6.2: "The Utopian Town of Celebration" 99
- SPEAKING: Living Environment 102
- LISTENING PRACTICE: Identify Contractions 103
- LISTENING: Littering 103
- SPEAKING: Public Service Announcement 104
- READING 6.3: "Chaos in the Streets" 105
- TAKE ACTION! 107
- REVISING AND EDITING 108

CHAPTER 7 Social Issues 110
- START UP: Crime Scenes 111
- LISTENING PRACTICE: Police Reports 112
- READING 7.1: "Flash Mobs, Flash Robs, and Riots" 113
- SPEAKING: Flash Mob 117
- LISTENING PRACTICE:
  1. Word Stress 117
  2. Word Stress in Sentences 118
- LISTENING: Public Shaming 118
- SPEAKING: Crime and Punishment 119
- READING 7.2: "The Cop and the Anthem" 121
- WATCHING: Ask Me Anything: I'm Homeless 126
- TAKE ACTION! 127
- REVISING AND EDITING 128

READING SUPPLEMENT: "Toggling the Switch" by Alicia Gifford 130

WRITING WORKSHOP 1: Writing a Paragraph 137
WRITING WORKSHOP 2: Writing an Essay 142
WRITING WORKSHOP 3: Improving Your Essay 149
WRITING WORKSHOP 4: Writing an Argument Essay 157

APPENDIX 1: Oral Presentations 159
APPENDIX 2: Idioms and Expressions 160
APPENDIX 3: Description Vocabulary 161
APPENDIX 4: Pronunciation 162
APPENDIX 5: Spelling, Grammar, and Vocabulary Logs 164

INDEX 165

PART 1
THE GOOD LIFE

CHAPTER 1

"Twenty years from now you will be more disappointed by the things that you didn't do than by the ones you did do. So sail away from the safe harbour. Catch the trade winds in your sails. Explore. Dream. Discover."
— MARK TWAIN, WRITER

On the Road

Why do people travel? What are some cultural differences travellers should be aware of? In this chapter, you will reflect on life on the road.

2	**START UP** International Crossword
4	**READING 1.1** Why I Travel
7	**LISTENING** Out-of-Control Travel Adventure
8	**SPEAKING** Body Language
9	**READING 1.2** Cultural Minefields
12	**WATCHING** Ocean Survival Part 1: Rip Currents Part 2: Tsunami
14	**READING 1.3** Record-Breaking Travel Adventure
17	**SPEAKING** Travel Interview
18	**TAKE ACTION!**
20	**REVISING AND EDITING**

START UP — International Crossword

Work with a partner. Look at the word clues to complete the crossword puzzle.

Rio de Janeiro

Across

1. The capital of ___ is Nairobi. (Barak Obama's father is from this country.)
3. Athens is the capital of ___.
6. This is the postal abbreviation for Saskatchewan.
7. The citizens of Ireland are ___.
10. Someone from Canada is ___.
11. ___ is directly south of the United States.
12. The Coliseum is in this Italian city.
13. This is the abbreviation for "rest and relaxation."
14. Bali is in ___.
15. In Europe, the citizens of ___ speak Spanish.
16. This tiny nation shares an island with the Dominican Republic.
17. The most prominent religion in ___ is Hinduism.

Down

1. ___ is a nickname for someone from New Zealand. (It is also the name of a fruit.)
2. This is the postal abbreviation for Alberta.
3. A person from Germany is ___.
4. There are 138 pyramids in ___.
5. Rio de Janeiro is in this large South American country.
6. This small European nation is known for its neutrality.
8. A person from Italy is ___.
9. The platypus and kangaroo live in ___.
12. Moscow is in this country.
14. In 2003, the United States invaded ___ and began a war. This country is next to Iran.
16. This is the postal abbreviation for Hawaii.

Mountain rice terrace, Bali

READING STRATEGY

Using Context Clues

1. **Look at the parts of the word.** You might recognize a part of the word and then be able to guess its meaning (for example, **door**knob).
2. **Determine the part of speech.** Sometimes it helps to know a word's function. Is it a noun, verb, adjective, etc.? For example, in the sentence "He received a fine," it helps to recognize that *fine* is a noun.
3. **Look at surrounding words and sentences.** Other words in the sentence can help you. Look for a **synonym** (a word that means the same thing) or **antonym** (a word that means the opposite). Also look at surrounding sentences. These may give you clues to the word's meaning.

Recognizing Cognates

Many different languages share words that have the same linguistic root. Cognates—or *word twins*—are words that have a similar appearance and meaning in different languages.

EXAMPLE: *English:* prove   *French:* prouver   *Spanish:* probar

False Cognates

Sometimes words in two languages appear to be similar, but they have completely different meanings. For example, the French word *pain* (meaning "bread") is a false cognate because it does not mean the same thing as the English word *pain* (meaning "physical or mental suffering").

Prepare for your reading tests by visiting the Companion Website. Click on "Reading Strategies" to find a variety of practice exercises.

PRACTICE

1. Work with a partner. Read the following paragraph and then write definitions for the words in **bold** in the spaces provided.

   These days, most North Americans have lives that **lack** excitement. Our distant ancestors faced **formidable** opponents: they **battled** wild **beasts** and engaged in tribal warfare. Today, I don't get the **chance** to be a hunter or a warrior. The most significant **hazard** I face is damage to my heart caused by **overeating** and inactivity.

   a. lack: _____
   b. formidable: _____
   c. battled: _____
   d. beasts: _____
   e. chance: _____
   f. hazard: _____
   g. overeating: *eating too much*

2. Which words in the paragraph are cognates? Write some true and false cognates on the lines.

   _____   _____
   _____   _____
   _____   _____

CHAPTER 1 | On the Road

READING 1.1

Ben Casnocha is a San Francisco-based entrepreneur and the author of *My Start Up Life*. He travels around the world for business. In the following blog from his website, he reflects on why he travels.

On the line next to each highlighted word, write a short definition, synonym, or translation. Use context clues to guess the meaning of each word.

Why I Travel

BY BEN CASNOCHA

EXAMPLE: leave or put

1 I travel because travelling makes me less afraid of the world. **Drop** me anywhere in the world, and I'll survive. I have lost any fear of other cultures. As I get to know citizens in other nations, I realize our basic similarities. For instance, in India, I met a mother who worried because her child was being ostracized and **teased** at school. In China, I befriended a shy student who really wanted to find a girlfriend. In Indonesia, I met a student who could not afford his education. He made the **sensible** decision to run a business on the side to help **fund** his studies. As I travel, I become less racist. Racism is something we have to un-learn.

2 I travel because travel enriches my internal mental stream. I think more original thoughts when I'm travelling; I think more critically about where I am and what I'm doing. My memory comes alive in interesting ways. In Beijing the other day, I **gazed** out at a huge lake and mountains, and the scene reminded me of standing at a cliff on the Kenai Peninsula in Alaska. I couldn't quite **recall** the Alaskan memory, but I felt the connection, and a tremendous stream of thoughts followed. Alain de Bottom says, "Few places are more conducive to internal conversations than a moving plane, ship, or train. There is an almost quaint correlation between what is in front of our eyes and the thoughts we are able to have in our heads: large thoughts requiring large views. Introspective reflections are helped along by the flow of the **landscape**."

3 I travel to force myself to live in the real world as opposed to in head-land. Familiar territory **dulls** my antenna to the world. When I go to my gym in San Francisco, I am unobservant. I've done the walk down the same street so many times that I mostly **stare** at the sidewalk and live within myself. When I'm in a new place, I have to pay attention to the street signs, and thus to everything else.

4 I travel to be anonymous. **Abroad**, I am not "Ben." In China, I am a foreign devil. In Latin America, I am a gringo. In Europe, I am, apparently, just another tall blond German. In Ukraine, I am an unmarried North American with the power to marry and immigrate my spouse. My individuality is subsumed by a group label and the associated stereotypes, and that is, in small **doses**, oddly liberating.

4 | PART 1 | The Good Life

5 I travel, not because it makes me happy in the moment—in fact, many moments are uncomfortable and stressful at the moment that I experience them—but because it makes me happy **afterwards**. I'm happy when I recall memories, embellish and share stories, and read articles in the newspaper and am able to say to myself, "I've been there."

6 Buying new experiences makes us happy; buying more things does not lift us. My **journeys** to other nations provide me with multiple gifts. I am grateful that I am able to indulge myself in travel. I am most grateful that I won't have regrets about not travelling when I'm older.

(519 words)

Source: Casnocha, Ben. "Ben Casnocha: A Blog." ben.casnotcha.com, 8 Sept. 2009. Web.

COMPREHENSION

1. Using your own words, list five things that Ben Casnocha learns when he travels.

_____
_____
_____
_____

GRAMMAR LINK

2. Look at the first sentence in paragraph 5, and underline the five verbs.

   a) Why does the first verb, *travel*, not end in –s?

   Because of "I"

   b) Why does *makes* end in –s?

   _____

3. a) In the first sentence of paragraph 6, what are the two subjects?

   _____

   b) Why do the two verbs end in –s? (See the Grammar Tip below.)

   _____

   c) In the first sentence of paragraph 6, what is the negative form of the verb *lift*?

   _____

 Answer additional reading and listening questions. You can also access audio and video clips online.

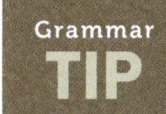

Third-Person Singular Subjects

In the simple present, when the subject is one person, place, or thing (but not *you* or *I*), the verb ends in –s or –es.

   Angela loves to travel.

Sometimes a gerund (the *–ing* form of a verb) can be the singular subject of a sentence.

   Travelling teaches us about other cultures.

To learn more about the present tenses, see Unit 2 in *Avenues 2: English Grammar*.

LISTENING PRACTICE

1. Pronounce –s on Verbs

When present tense verbs follow a third-person singular subject, the verb ends in –s or –es. There are two different ways to pronounce the final ending.

Pronunciation TIP

THIRD-PERSON SINGULAR

Most verbs end in an –s sound.

EXAMPLES: write   writes   hope   hopes

Add –es to a verb ending in –s, –ch, –sh, –x, or –z. Pronounce the final –es as a separate syllable.

EXAMPLES: wash   washes [washiz]   reach   reaches [reachiz]

Practise your spelling by doing dictations.

You will hear the third-person singular form of each verb. Say each verb twice. Then indicate if the verb ends with an –s, a –z, or an –iz sound.

1st person - I
2nd person - You
3rd person - He, She, It

1	claps	(s)	z	iz	8	forces	s	z	(iz)
2	pushes	s	z	(iz)	9	laughs	(s)	z	iz
3	coughs	(s)	z	iz	10	asks	(s)	z	iz
4	sneezes	s	z	(iz)	11	races	s	z	(iz)
5	believes	s	(z)	iz	12	tries	(s)	z	iz
6	hopes	(s)	z	iz	13	fixes	s	z	(iz)
7	touches	s	z	(iz)	14	teaches	s	z	(iz)

2. Pronounce Complete Sentences

Listen to the sentences and repeat each sentence after the speaker. Then fill in the blanks with the words that you hear. You can use contracted forms.

EXAMPLE: Lauren _travels_ every summer.

1. Travel _____ people to appreciate other cultures.
2. A traveller _____ how people live in other places.
3. Lauren _____ three languages.
4. She _____ German.
5. Right now, she _____ at a map.
6. Lauren has allergies, so she often _____.
7. At this moment, she _____.
8. Every Wednesday, Pedro _____ to work.
9. He _____ a car.
10. Pedro and Lauren _____ to visit Peru next summer.

Out-of-Control Travel Adventure

CBC's *DNTO* host Sook Yin-Lee interviews Alex Sabine about her travel adventure. Listen to the interview.

VOCABULARY

1 Listen to the introduction to the interview and fill in the missing words. Use the following terms.

daydream   goal   road
does   interviews   voted

Do you ever __daydream__ about getting into your car and going somewhere far away? __Does__ an unplanned road trip sound exciting? Well, in 2009, Alex Sabine and her best friend Luke decided to hit the __road__. They used the power of social media to help them discover North America. Their __goal__ was to visit every state, province, and territory. Every day, ordinary people logged onto their website and __voted__ on where Luke and Sabine should go next. Listen as CBC radio host Sook Yin-Lee __interviews__ Alex Sabine about her travel adventure.

Luke and Alex

COMPREHENSION

2 When did Alex Sabine work on her thesis in London? __2008__ 2008

3 Why did she leave London?
__Broke up w/ boyfriend. Returned to Canada.__

4 What happened when she moved back home to Canada?
a. Her family home burned down.
b. She got a job, but before she could begin, she lost the job.
(c.) Both a and b

5 In West Virginia, what activity did Sabine try?
a. skydiving
b. scuba diving
(c.) whitewater rafting

6 What was Sabine's opinion of her adventure in West Virginia?
__1 of best things she's ever done.__

7 How did Sabine "give up control" of her travel adventure?
__It gave her control. Changed her personality and took risk__

8 How has the travel experience changed her?
(a.) She has learned to grab life and enjoy experiences.
b. She has learned that she really wants to sell art at Christie's.
c. She has learned that she loves Luke.

SPEAKING

Body Language

Work with a partner. Put the appropriate verbs in the spaces provided. Use the *-ing* form of each verb.

| bow ✓ | hug ✓ | point | sip ✓ | wave ✓ |
| crouch/duck | lean ✓ | shrug ✓ | snap ✓ | wink ✓ |

EXAMPLE: They **are hugging**.

1. She *is sipping* her coffee.

2. She *is waving* at someone.

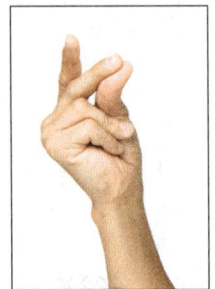

3. He *is snapping* his fingers.

4. He *is shrugging*.

5. He *is leaning* against the wall.

6. She *is winking*.

7. They *are bowing*.

8. He *is crouching*.
9. She _____.

Grammar TIP

Present Progressive

When you describe an action that is happening now, use the correct form of *be* + the *-ing* form of the verb.

The woman **is pointing** at the man.   They **are** not **laughing**.

To learn more about the present tenses, see Unit 2 in *Avenues 2: English Grammar*.

READING 1.2

When you travel, there are a variety of gestures and actions that can easily be misinterpreted. Read the following newspaper article about some cultural minefields.

PRE-READING VOCABULARY

The following expressions appear in "Cultural Minefields." Guess the meaning of the expressions. Write the letters of the correct definitions in the spaces beside them. Then read the essay. The paragraph numbers are in parentheses.

Expressions		Definitions
1. hailed a taxi (1)	d	a. the general rule
2. a hush fell over the room (1)	e	b. see things in opposite ways
3. shot me a dirty look (1)	f	c. have a better understanding of the world
4. be worlds apart (2)	b	d. signalled for a taxi
5. the rule of thumb (8)	a	e. the place became quiet
6. broaden your mind (11)	c	f. looked at me with contempt

Cultural Minefields

BY WILLIAM ECENBARGER

1 In Sydney, Australia, I simply hailed a taxi, opened the door, and jumped in the back seat. The driver narrowed his eyes. "Where to, mate?" he asked in a voice that could chill a refrigerator. In Marrakech, Morocco, I crossed my legs during an interview with a government official. Immediately, a hush fell over the room. In a restaurant in Mumbai, India, all I did was reach for the nan. A diner at the next table shot me a dirty look.

2 It took years before I realized what I'd done. It turns out that in each case I had, unwittingly, committed a *faux pas*. To varying degrees, I had offended my hosts. My only comfort is my ignorance. I take solace in Oscar Wilde's observation that a gentleman is someone who never gives offence—unintentionally. And after nearly twenty-five years of travel on six continents, I have learned the hard way that getting through customs is a lot more difficult than just filling out a declaration form. It means navigating a series of cultural **booby traps**. It means understanding that although people everywhere are the same biologically, they can be worlds apart in their habits and traditions. Here's my advice for anyone visiting another country: Eat, drink—and be wary.

booby trap: a device or trick that catches an unsuspecting victim

3 My Australian taxi driver was offended because I sat in the back seat rather than up front next to him. His attitude is not uncommon, according to *Kiss, Bow or Shake Hands*, a book on business behaviour, and it stems from Australians' disdain of class distinctions.

4 My interview with the Moroccan bureaucrat was cut short because, in crossing my legs, I had showed him the sole of one of my shoes, a grave affront to Muslims who see the foot as unclean.

5 I reached for the bread in Mumbai. There's nothing wrong with this per se, but I did it with my left hand. Indians eat with their hands, in particular their right. Their left hands are reserved for other matters, including after-toilet cleansing, and are therefore unacceptable for use at the dining table.

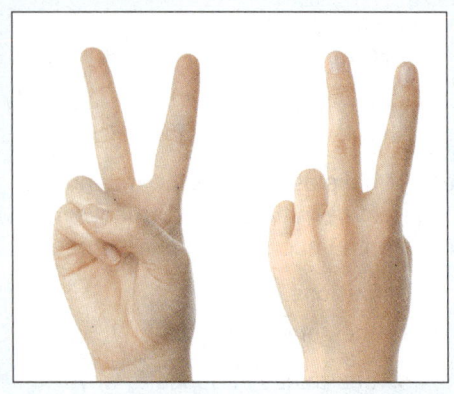

6. When I curled my thumb and index finger into a circle and pointed the other three fingers upward, my intention was to tell the Brazilian hotel clerk that everything was "OK." That would have worked fine at home in the US, but in Brazil, it is considered vulgar because it refers to the anus. The OK sign is not OK in many other places too, including most of the rest of Latin America, plus Germany, Malta, Tunisia, Greece, Turkey, Russia, and the Middle East.

7. There are many hand gestures that don't travel well. The "V" for victory sign was immortalized by Winston Churchill in the early, dark days of World War II, and the proper form is with the palm facing outward. A simple twist of the wrist puts you in dangerous cultural waters. Throughout much of Her Majesty's realm, the palm-in V sign is the equivalent of the more infamous middle-digit salute. During the Middle Ages, it was thought that French soldiers would permanently disarm English **bowmen** by cutting off their middle and index fingers, the ones they used to draw the bowstring. Consequently, the English were said to celebrate battlefield victories and taunt the French by displaying these two digits intact.

bowmen: men who used bows and arrows

take this and shove it: vulgar expression that basically means, "I'm really angry with you, so go away."

8. Even though the "thumbs up" gesture (meaning everything is fine) has worldwide acceptance among many pilots, it can get you in big trouble outside the cockpit. If you're hitchhiking in Nigeria, for example, your upraised thumb may be interpreted as a **take-this-and-shove-it** insult to passing motorists. In parts of the Middle East, it is an invitation for sexual relations. The rule of thumb is, don't do it.

9. Sometimes I think the solution is to tie my hands behind my back, but there are countless other ways to offend while travelling. The entire area of food and drink is a cultural minefield. In Asia, for example, you would never leave your chopsticks upright in your food. As Chin-ning Chu, author of *The Asian Mind Game*, advises, "It is a common Asian superstition that to place your chopsticks in such a way is bad luck and means that this meal is for the dead rather than the living."

10. When drinking with others in Prague, Czech Republic, before the first sip, the Czechs deem it important to look their companions in the eye and lightly clink glasses. Less than 482 kilometres away in Budapest, Hungary, however, that identical gesture can get you deep in goulash. The clink is considered unpatriotic because it was once the signal for a coup.

11. Travel won't broaden you unless your mind is broad to begin with. After all, a foreign country isn't designed to make the traveller comfortable; it's designed to make its own people comfortable.

(807 words)

Source: Ecenbarger, William. "A Cultural Minefield." *Los Angeles Times*. Los Angeles Times, 17 Apr. 2008. Web.

COMPREHENSION

1. A minefield is an area where explosive devices are hidden in the ground. A mine may explode if an unsuspecting victim steps on one. Why is the text called "Cultural Minefields"?

   _____
   _____

2. In paragraph 2, what does *unwittingly* mean?
   a. purposely; intentionally
   (b.) accidentally; unintentionally

3. At the end of paragraph 2, what is the meaning of *wary*?
   a. alone   b. happy   (c.) careful

4. In paragraph 8, find a word that means "the small room where pilots control the airplane." _____

Answer the following questions based on material in the text.

5. You are in Sydney, Australia, and you just called a cab. You get into the back seat. Now the driver is annoyed with you. Why?
   a. You did not wait for him to open the door. You seemed rude.
   b. You did not offer him money before you opened the door.
   (c.) You sat in the back seat and not the front seat. You insulted the driver by making him feel like he's inferior to you.

6. This man is insulting his host in Morocco. What is he doing?
   a. He is not wearing a tie.
   (b.) He is pointing the sole of his shoe at his host.
   c. He is looking directly at his host.

7. In India, this man is doing something very distasteful and disgusting. What mistake is he making?
   a. Peanuts are sacred in India, and he is eating peanut butter.
   (b.) He is eating with his left hand. In India, the left hand is considered dirty.
   c. His sandwich is missing the top piece of bread.

8. What does this "thumbs up" gesture mean in parts of the Middle East?
   a. Everything is alright.
   b. I hate you.
   (c.) I want to make love with you.

9. Never clink glasses in a toast. The gesture is unpatriotic because it was once the signal for a coup. In which country is this notion true?
   a. Czech Republic
   b. Australia
   (c.) Hungary

10. In your own words, explain how people can avoid cultural misunderstandings.

    _____
    _____

Travel Terms

The following terms and expressions relate to travel. Review them and then complete the paragraphs.

book: reserve
border: dividing line between two countries
hit the road: start a trip
round trip: trip to a destination and back home
travel lightly: travel with very little luggage
vacancy: unoccupied room in a hotel, motel, etc.
vacation: holiday

PRACTICE

Fill in the blanks. Use a different word or expression in each blank. Choose from the list of words above.

1. I plan to _hit the road_ next month because I will have a one-week _vacation_. I am travelling to Vermont. I always _travel lightly_ and do not bring much luggage with me.

2. I will need to bring my passport because I am going to cross the Canada/US _border_. I will not _book_ a hotel in advance. I hope that when I arrive in Stowe, there is a _vacancy_ sign in front of a cheap hotel. I can't afford an expensive hotel.

Ocean Survival

PART ONE: RIP CURRENTS

Large bodies of water sometimes have very strong rip tides, which can be dangerous. Watch this video and learn how to save yourself if you ever find yourself caught in an undertow.

PRE-WATCHING VOCABULARY

Before you watch the video, review the following vocabulary terms.

- **rip current (also called a "rip tide" or an "undertow"):** an unusually strong current that can pull someone out to sea
- **pond:** a small body of water
- **sand bar:** a bar or ridge of sand that is formed in a body of water
- **wave:** the undulating ridge of water that moves toward the shore

COMPREHENSION

1. At the beginning of the video, where are the speakers?
   a. Walton County, Florida ✓
   b. Los Angeles, California
   c. Miami Beach, Florida

2. How many people died on the beach on "Black Sunday" in 2003?
   a. three   b. five   c. eight ✓

3. Where do rip currents occur?
   a. only in oceans
   b. in any ocean or lake where there is a sandbar ✓

4. What causes a rip current? Number the steps from 1 to 4.
   - _3_ The sand bar develops a break or opening.
   - _2_ A pond forms because the sand bar blocks the water from incoming waves.
   - _1_ A complete sand bar forms.
   - _4_ The water in the pond rushes through the break in the sandbar.

5. On this drawing, explain what you should do if you are caught in a rip current. With arrows, show where you should swim.

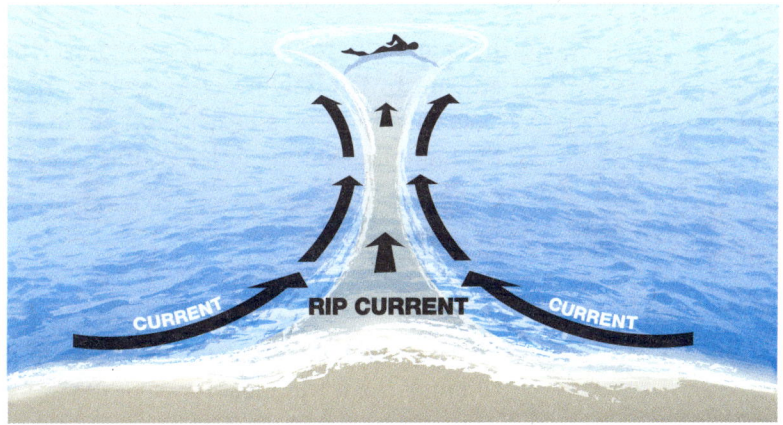

PART TWO: TSUNAMI

In December 2004, Tilly Smith and her family were vacationing in Thailand. Tilly noticed something odd about the ocean. Watch and find out what happened.

COMPREHENSION

6. How old was Tilly Smith in 2004?
   _10_

7. Why did Tilly believe that there was a tsunami coming?
   She had studied it in school

8. Tilly warned her parents about the tsunami survival. How did her parents react?
_____
_____

9. Someone confirmed Tilly's tsunami theory. Who was it?
   a. the security guard   b. Tilly's dad   c. a Japanese tourist

10. After Tilly first noticed the strange water, how long did it take for the guard to start evacuating the beach?
    a. ten minutes   b. fifteen minutes   c. thirty minutes

11. How high was the wall of water that came toward the shore?
    30'

12. At Tilly's hotel, did everyone survive?   ☑ Yes   ☐ No

READING 1.3

Some people are born thrill seekers. Read about an adventure traveller. Graham Hughes details his adventures on his blog *theodysseyexpedition.com*.

Record-Breaking Travel Adventure

INTERVIEW WITH GRAHAM HUGHES

1. Travellers fit into some clear categories. There are the organized-tour types who attempt to see Italy in fourteen days. The all-inclusive traveller wants nothing more than to lie on a beach, a mojito in hand. Some backpackers strive to climb the highest mountain or break other world records.

2. Graham Hughes is an adventure traveller and filmmaker from Liverpool, England. In 2009, he decided to break a world record by travelling to every sovereign state in the world ... without flying. He's been filming his adventures for *National Geographic*. *Avenues* asked Hughes some questions.

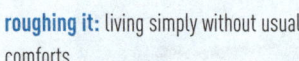
roughing it: living simply without usual comforts

3. **Visiting two hundred countries overland is a challenge. Why did you decide to break the world record?**

4. I wanted to capture people's imaginations and inspire them to travel themselves. I'm good at travelling—I can read maps, I can sleep anywhere, I don't mind **roughing it**, and I hardly ever get ill—so if there was a world record I knew I could achieve, it was this one.

5. **What were some of the risks?**

6. The majority of my travels have been incredibly enjoyable, but I did end up in jail twice. The first time, I was arrested in the Cape Verde islands off the west coast of Africa. I had convinced a group of Senegalese fishermen to bring me there on their fishing boat. When I arrived in Cape Verde, the police thought I was people-smuggling. We were all put in a cell with no beds or windows, and the toilet was a hole in the ground. I spent six days being detained before our case came to court and we were released. However, they refused to let us go back to Senegal in the canoe, so the fishermen were flown back home, and I waited for six weeks before a kindly German sailor rescued me from the islands.

7. A few months later I was in Congo, and I was having a terrible time crossing the country. I hitched a ride in a truck that was doubling as a

Graham Hughes on the border of the Central African Republic

bus service, and I arrived in the capital city, Brazzaville, just after dark. At a checkpoint on the edge of town, the police found videotapes in my bag and decided that I must be a spy. I spent six days in a squalid police cell protesting my innocence. The police took everything—my T-shirt, my shoes, and socks—even my glasses. Eventually, a man from the the British Honorary Consulate managed to get me out, but only after the chief of police watched every videotape in my bag.

8 As I crossed the threshold of my prison cell, I donned my hat, and I jumped into my rescuer's car. I was whisked away to his house, where his wife was waiting to greet me with a bottle of Baileys by the swimming pool. It was like crawling through a sewer and finding yourself at a cocktail party.

9 **What was your most frightening experience?**

400 miles: about 645 kilometres

sails: canvas sheets that capture the wind and move a boat forward

oars: long shafts with a wide, flat blade at one end used to steer a boat through the water

10 The most terrifying experience was taking the leaky wooden canoe from Senegal to Cape Verde. It took three days to get there, **400 miles** over open ocean. The Senegalese fishermen didn't know any English. We had no GPS, no radio, no satellite phone, no flares, no **sails**, and no **oars**. I even had to buy my own life jacket. If the outboard motor had broken, we would be dead. If a rogue wave hit us, we would be dead. If I fell overboard, I'd be dead. It was three days and three nights of sheer terror, the scariest thing I've ever done, although leaping off the massive 135-metre Nevis Highwire bungee jump in New Zealand comes a close second.

11 **What was one of the most memorable places you visited?**

12 Iran was a real eye-opener. It was nothing like what I thought it would be. From the moment I crossed the border, I was amazed at how incredibly friendly everybody was. It was wonderful.

Graham Hughes on the triple border of Cameroon, Gabon, and Equatorial Guinea

13 The most touching thing that's happened to me occurred on the bus from Shiraz. A little old lady—she must have been in her nineties—was sitting in front of me. She didn't speak a word of English, but she turned around and offered me her phone, gesturing for me to listen to it. I put the phone to my ear and the man on the other end introduced himself as Hossein. He explained that he was an English teacher and that I was sitting behind his grandmother. "She's concerned that the bus is going to arrive very early, at 5 a.m., and that you're not going to have any breakfast. She wants you to come to her home so she can make you something to eat. Would that be okay?" I gratefully accepted Granny's offer. She laid out a Persian breakfast fit for a king.

14 If you want any more proof that the Iranians are the most beautiful people on the planet, I humbly suggest you visit the place yourself. Iran has gone straight into my top ten countries in the world. The most valuable thing I'm learning while travelling around the world is that the vast majority of people are good, trustworthy souls—many of whom will bend over backwards to help you out. It really *is* a wonderful world.

15 **This must be costing a fortune! Are you rich?**

16 Far from it! I couch surf, and I don't stay at hotels that cost more than $10 a night. Also, nearly all the boat rides have been free—the boat was going there anyway! I eat cheap street food. I don't own any property; I don't have a mortgage or any dependents.

17 In short, you can do this! If you can't find anybody to go with, go by yourself—you're never alone for long. And backpacking is not expensive! Give up the cigs, man—that'll save you a fiver a day. Don't waste your money on DVDs that you'll never watch, mobile ringtones, lottery tickets, or clothes that you'll never wear. Your Canadian passport is an "Access All Areas" pass to the world. Use it!

(989 words)

COMPREHENSION

For questions 1 to 5, read the words in context before you make your guess.

1. What is *people-smuggling*? Look in paragraph 6 and make a guess.
   _____

2. Find a three-word expression in paragraph 7 that means "received a lift from a passing vehicle." ___hitchhike___

3. Find a word in paragraph 7 that means "dirty; repulsive." ___squalid___

4. In paragraph 8, what does *donned* mean?
   a. (put on)
   b. opened
   c. left

5. In paragraph 12, Hughes refers to Iran as an *eye opener*. What does he mean?
   ___country___

6. Guess the meaning of the expression *bend over backwards*. See paragraph 14. _____

7. Why did Hughes end up in jail twice? List both reasons.
   _____
   _____

8. What surprised Hughes about Iran?
   _____

9. At the end of the essay, he says, "Give up the cigs, man—that'll save you a fiver a day." What does he mean, in plain English?
   _____

10. What is his concluding suggestion?
    _____
    _____

GRAMMAR LINK

11. Look in paragraph 1, and underline the four main verbs in the first three sentences. Do not underline infinitives, which are verbs that follow *to*. Write the subjects and verbs below.

Subjects	Verbs	Subjects	Verbs
Travellers	fit	types	attempt
There	are	traveller	wants

12 In paragraph 1, why does the second sentence begin with *There are* instead of *There is*?

DISCUSSION

Hughes risks his life crossing to Cape Verde on a small boat. He spends three days and nights fearing for his life. Why do people like Hughes risk their lives? What do they probably gain from the experience? Would you risk your life for travel adventures?

SPEAKING — Travel Interview

Work with a partner and complete the following tasks.
- Add the missing word (*do*, *does*, *is*, or *are*) in each question.
- Write your partner's answers in the spaces provided. You can write words or phrases.

Before you begin, remember the following:
Travel is usually used as a verb. You travel to another place.
Trip is a noun. You take a trip somewhere.

EXAMPLE: Where _do_ you live?   Answer: _in Montreal_

Partner's name: (Mr. / Mrs. / Ms.) _____
                                       first name   last name

Birthplace: _____

To Be
I am   We are
You are   They are
He is

Do
I do   We do
You do   They do
He does

1 How old __are__ you?
Answer: _____

2 What __is__ your nationality?
Answer: _He is 19 years old_

3 How many languages __do__ you speak fluently?
a. one   b. two   c. three   d. more than three
List the languages: _____

4 What __are__ your two strongest language skills in English? (Circle the answers.)
speaking   listening   reading   writing

5 Why __is__ it useful to know other languages? Think of at least two reasons.
Answer: _____

6 What __do__ you do each summer during your vacation?
Answer: _____

7 Which countries _____ you want to visit? List at least two places.

Answer (explain why): _____
_____
_____

8 What type of traveller _____ you? Choose the type of traveller you are or you would like to be in the future.

   a. backpacker (stay in youth hostels and couch surf)
   b. camper (stay in a tent)
   c. planned-itinerary traveller (travel with a group and stay in hotels)
   d. all-inclusive traveller (stay in hotels with food and drinks included)

9 _____ you a thrill seeker?

Explain your answer: _____
_____
_____

10 _____ any of your friends take dangerous risks?

Explain your answer: _____
_____
_____

WRITING

Write about your partner in a paragraph of about 100 words. Use some information from the "Travel Interview." Remember to add –s or –es endings to present tense verbs that follow third-person singular subjects.

EXAMPLE: He want**s** to visit Greece.

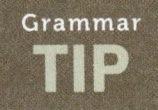

Capitalization

Notice that languages and nationalities are always capitalized in English.

Octavio is **M**exican, and he speaks **S**panish and **E**nglish.

To learn more about capitalization, see Unit 11 in *Avenues 2: English Grammar*.

Take Action!

WRITING TOPICS

Write about one of the following topics. For information about paragraph and essay structure, see the Writing Workshops on pages 137 to 148. Before handing in your work, refer to the Writing Checklist on the inside back cover.

1 My Country

What are the advantages of living in your country? (You can discuss the country you currently live in or the country you were born in.)

2. A Meaningful Holiday or Ceremony

Why do all cultures have special holidays and ceremonies? In your answer, provide specific examples of holidays or ceremonies that you have witnessed. For example, you can describe a wedding or funeral, or you can describe a religious or national holiday such as Christmas, Hanukah, or Valentine's Day.

3. Travel

Explain why people travel. Give two or three reasons, and provide examples from your life or the lives of people you know.

4. Survival Lessons

Should schools teach students about survival skills? Why or why not? Provide at least two reasons for your opinion. You can include examples from the ocean survival video.

SPEAKING TOPICS

Prepare a presentation about one of the following topics.

1. Thrill Seekers

Explain why people do dangerous activities such as car surfing or mountain climbing. Give two reasons. Provide examples of people you know who take many risks.

2. Volunteer Tourism

Did you or someone you know do volunteer work in another country? Present information about the work and the trip to your classmates.

3. Local Tourism Project

Your region is trying to convince tourists to visit. Prepare a short advertisement (one to two minutes long) about one of the following topics. Remember that your audience is people from other countries. You are trying to attract tourists, so make the place, weather, food, etc., sound very appealing.

- Give advice to people who are visiting your area. What should they pack? What is the weather like? How do people greet each other? What are the local people's attitudes? What are typical greetings in English and in other languages?
- Describe an interesting place in your region. Choose somewhere that you know well. Explain why it is an appealing place to visit.
- Describe the local cuisine. Choose some types of food that are popular in your region. Explain how to make the food and/or describe good places to find it.
- Describe a celebration or holiday that is popular in your area. What do people do for the celebration? Explain the cultural significance of the celebration.

■ VOCABULARY REVIEW

Review key terms from this chapter. Identify any words that you do not understand and learn their meanings.

- ☐ book (v.)
- ☐ duck (v.)
- ☐ hitchhike
- ☐ journey
- ☐ landscape
- ☐ lean
- ☐ thrill
- ☐ tide
- ☐ trip
- ☐ vacancy
- ☐ vacation
- ☐ wave (v. and n.)

To practise vocabulary from this chapter, visit the Companion Website.

SPEAKING PRESENTATION TIPS

- **PRACTISE YOUR PRESENTATION** and time yourself. You should speak for about three minutes or for a length determined by your teacher.
- **USE CUE CARDS.** Do not read! Put about fifteen keywords on your cue cards.
- **BRING VISUAL SUPPORT** such as an object, drawing, poster, photograph, or PowerPoint presentation, or create a short video.
- **CLASSMATES WILL ASK YOU QUESTIONS** about your presentation. You must also ask classmates about their presentations. Review how to form questions before your presentation day.

Revising and Editing

REVISE FOR A MAIN IDEA

The following paragraph contains supporting details, but it has no main idea. The main idea is expressed in a topic sentence. Read the paragraph and then add a good topic sentence. (For more information about topic sentences, see Writing Workshop 1, page 138.)

Topic sentence: _____

_____

First, it is a good idea to do a background check on the volunteer organization before you commit to it. Some volunteer travel organizations charge participants a high fee. According to CBC reporter Wallace Immen, "There are less-than-altruistic groups that exploit free labour." Also, consider your skills. Decide what talent you can bring to your volunteer position. Do you want to build houses in India? Would you like to teach children in Africa? Finally, be prepared to live simply. It is annoying for those you are trying to help if you walk around with your iPod, iPad, and other expensive gadgets, continually reminding the locals that they can't afford such things.

EDIT PRESENT TENSE VERBS AND WORD CHOICE

Practise editing a student paragraph. Underline and correct five errors with present tense verbs, not including the example. Also correct two word-choice errors.

           travel
People <u>travels</u> for many reasons. During the summer vacancy, many workers need a break, and they want to spend time with their families. For instance, my family stay at my uncle's cottage each summer. We only make one travel to the cottage, and we stay for about ten days. Other people travel for their jobs. Marco, my neighbour, visit many cities for his work. He often is complaining because he don't like to stay in hotels. Everyone travel for different reasons.

Simple Present or Present Progressive

Use the simple present to discuss facts, habits, or customs. Use the present progressive only when an action is currently in progress.

                  doesn't travel
Melanie <u>is not travelling</u> every summer because she always works.

To learn more about the present tenses, see Unit 2 in *Avenues 2: English Grammar*.

"Most people pursue pleasure with such breathless haste that they hurry past it."
– SOREN KIERKEGAARD, PHILOSOPHER

CHAPTER 2

The Pleasure Principle

What makes you laugh? What do you do to feel better about yourself? In this chapter, you will read about the things people do in their pursuit of pleasure and happiness.

22	**START UP** Simple Pleasures
23	**LISTENING** Awesome Things
25	**READING 2.1** The Botched Tan
27	**SPEAKING** Pleasure
28	**READING 2.2** Winter Love
31	**SPEAKING** Strong Emotions
32	**READING 2.3** Act Happy
35	**SPEAKING** The Greatest Country
35	**WATCHING** Living in Denmark
36	**TAKE ACTION!**
38	**REVISING AND EDITING**

START UP — Simple Pleasures

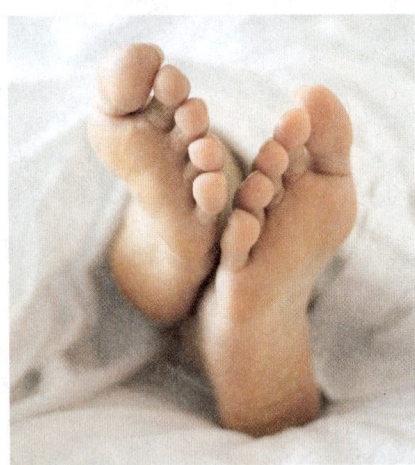

In 2008, after Neil Pasricha endured some personal setbacks, he started blogging about small everyday moments that make life better. Below are some awesome moments. Work with a partner and add at least three ideas to the list.

1. Waking up before your alarm clock and realizing you have lots of sleep time left
2. The first shower you take after not showering for a really long time
3. The sound of rain from inside the tent
4. Turning over the pillow while you're sleeping
5. Finding money that you did not know you had lost

WRITING

Write a paragraph of about 100 words about an awesome moment. Explain what happened. Use descriptive words.

LISTENING PRACTICE

1. Identify Silent Letters

Repeat each pair of words after the speaker. Then identify the silent letter in each pair of words. (For rules about silent letters, and for other pronunciation tips, see Appendix 4.)

Practise your spelling by doing dictations.

			Silent Letter	
EXAMPLE:	knit	know	<u>k</u>	n
1	hour	honest	(h)	o
2	knife	knowledge	k	(n)
3	castle	listen	s	(t)
4	design	benign	(g)	n
5	would	could	(l)	d
6	calm	palm	l	m
7	thumb	climb	m	(b)
8	write	wrong	(w)	r
9	walk	talk	(l)	k
10	psycho	psychedelic	(p)	s

PART 1 | The Good Life

2. Pronounce *gh*

Gh can have many pronunciations.
- *Gh* can be silent as in *through*.
- *Gh* can sound like *g* as in *ghost*.
- *Gh* can sound like *f* as in *laugh*.

Repeat each sentence after the speaker. Then indicate what *gh* sounds like.

		Gh sound		
1	Women **fought** for equal rights.	g	f	<u>silent</u>
2	I need to buy **cough** syrup.	g	<u>f</u>	silent
3	We make bread with **dough**.	g	f	<u>silent</u>
4	I **thought** that I knew him.	g	f	<u>silent</u>
5	Please don't **laugh**.	g	<u>f</u>	silent
6	Many people live in the **ghetto**.	<u>g</u>	f	silent
7	The shelf is very **high**.	g	f	<u>silent</u>
8	My skin is quite **rough**.	g	<u>f</u>	silent
9	Carrie **taught** when she was younger.	g	f	<u>silent</u>
10	Many people believe in **ghosts**.	<u>g</u>	f	silent

LISTENING: Awesome Things

On June 20, 2008, Neil Pasricha started his blog, *1000awesomethings.com*. His site has millions of fans. Soon after, publishers contacted him, and his first book, *The Book of Awesome*, became an international best-seller. Now, Pasricha has a new book. Listen as he discusses his decision to write about awesome moments.

COMPREHENSION

1. What two events made Pasricha decide to create his awesome blog?

   bad marriage, wife didn't love him anymore
   depressed friend, Chris, committed suicide

2. What is the name of his new book?
   a. *1000 Awesome Things*
   (b.) *The Book of Awesome*
   (c.) *The Book of (Even More) Awesome*

3. How long was his first book #1 on the best-seller list? _____

4. What are his books about?

   awesome things

5. When Pasricha was twenty years old, what did he want for his future?
   a. children
   b. a wife
   c. a house with a picket fence
   (d.) all of the answers

6 How old is Pasricha now? __31__

7 Does his life today match his expectations when he was 20? ☐ Yes ☑ No

8 Why does he continue to work at Walmart?
life stays same

9 How often does he add something to his website? __daily__

10 Pasricha mentions many "awesome moments" during the interview. What are two or three awesome moments that he mentions?
steak on grill
roommate leaves for wkend.
leftover cake in office kitchen

READING STRATEGY

Using a Dictionary

If you are unable to understand the meaning of a word by using context clues, you can look up the word in a dictionary. Review the following tips for proper dictionary usage.

- **Look at the preface and notes** in your dictionary. The preface contains explanations about the various symbols and abbreviations that appear throughout the dictionary. Find out what your dictionary has to offer.
- **Read all the definitions** listed for the word that you look up. Look for the meaning that best fits the context of the sentence in question.
- **Determine the part of speech**. For instance, imagine that you do not know what *tripped* means in the sentence, "Eric tripped and hurt himself." Your dictionary has definitions of *trip* (n.) and *trip* (v.). You would look at the verb definition.
- **Look at the parts of the word**. Determine if there is a prefix or suffix that can help you understand the word's meaning. For instance, the prefixes *un-*, *dis-*, and *il-* mean "not." The prefix *multi-* means "many," and the prefix *anti-* means "against." The suffix *-less* means "without."

Prepare for your reading tests by visiting the Companion Website. Click on "Reading Strategies" to find a variety of practice exercices.

PRACTICE

Use your dictionary or an online dictionary website such as *dictionary.reference.com* or *longmandictionariesonline.com*. Provide short definitions or synonyms for the words in bold. Check all the definitions and consider the part of speech before you write your definition.

1 The young woman said **mean** things and bullied her classmate. _____

2 I was making a joke and did not **mean** to insult her. _____

3 The Forsythes don't have the **means** to pay their rent. _____

4 Do you know what the word *shortage* **means**? _____

READING 2.1 Many people believe that changing their appearance will improve their lives. In the following essay, Sarah Stanfield describes her decision to change the colour of her skin by tanning. As you read, consider the meaning of the words in green. After you read, you will be asked to define those words.

The Botched Tan

BY SARAH STANFIELD

host family: family that provides room and board

mousy-brown: drab and ugly colour

gringos: Spanish word meaning foreigners (especially Americans)

1. Baños, Ecuador, is a **balmy** village on the neck of the massive Tungurahua volcano. Normally, I would be thrilled to be there, but instead, I was half-conscious with pain. Baños was supposed to be my first stop on a trek into the Amazon rain forest. Thanks to what I would later find out were second-degree burns on my legs, it became my last stop.

2. I was living in Quito as part of my university's study abroad program, conducting anthropological fieldwork for my senior thesis. A few days before, I had accompanied my **host family** to its relatives' ranch just outside the city. The place had a pool, and the cloudy sky convinced me it was the perfect day to change my pale skin to brown, no sunscreen needed. Quito rises about 9,000 feet above sea level. At this elevation, the atmosphere is thinner, making skin more vulnerable to the sun's rays. I knew this, but convinced myself the clouds in the sky would **temper** the intensity of the sun. So I stretched out next to the pool with a novel, rising four hours later with legs the colour of smoked salmon.

3. All my previous sunbathing efforts had resulted in a shade of red across my skin. Yet I kept striving for the miracle day when I would achieve a bronze glow. In Ecuador, almost everyone is of mixed Spanish and indigenous ancestry, with brown eyes, thick, glossy black hair, and olive skin. Looks-wise, they were everything I was not, with my **sallow** skin and my **mousy-brown** hair.

4. I was surprised when, shortly after my arrival, Diana, my fifteen-year-old host sister, complimented me on my "good skin." At first, I thought she was referring to my lack of acne. But then she ran her hand through my hair and said, "Good hair, too." She grabbed a chunk of her own hair and made a face. At first, I figured this to be typical teen-girl self-criticism. But eventually I realized it was much more **widespread**.

5. Ecuador has plenty of its own image complexes. Skin-lightening creams fill pharmacy shelves, and billboards depict smiling **gringos**. Matinee idols are mostly American movie stars. Of course, Ecuadorians are not alone in aspiring to gringo beauty ideals. The most notorious example of this is Xuxa, the tall blond Brazilian singer whose fans are of mixed African, Amerindian, and European ancestry.

6. I wasn't thinking about this as I took the bus ride from Quito to Baños, though. I was just feeling pain. For the first three days, I couldn't walk at all, and now my legs were covered with dime-size **blisters**. I hoped my skin would fade from red to brown. But when the bus suddenly lurched forward, my right leg bumped the scratchy surface of the seat in front of me. One of the blisters tore open, leaking burning fluid down my leg. Its **sting** convinced me that this was serious. I needed medical attention.

CHAPTER 2 | The Pleasure Principle | 25

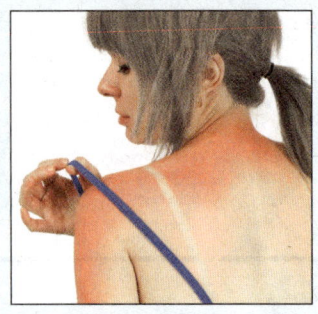

7. In Baños, I headed straight to the medical clinic. Meanwhile, my blisters were growing and were the size of quarters. In a tiny examination room, a young woman in a nurse's uniform greeted me. Her skin was the exact shade of caramel I yearned for. She was strikingly beautiful, except for her hair colour. It was the strained yellow of a botched bleach job.

8. I lifted my skirt to my thighs, displaying my blisters and explaining in Spanish what had happened. The nurse sucked in her breath and made a little clicking sound, shaking her head. "We'll need to pop the blisters and disinfect them," she said. "Then you need to go back to Quito and go to the hospital. This looks like a second-degree burn." She took out a bottle of alcohol, a needle, and some cotton balls.

9. With that, she got to work. **Tears** brimmed up in my eyes. Over and over I felt the needle, then the burning as the fluid **dribbled** out, and then the sting of alcohol on open **wounds**. The pain alone was enough for me to **swear** never again to go near a beach or tanning salon. But it was the comment from the nurse, as she finished her task, which made me realize the insanity of what I had done. Screwing the cap back on the bottle of alcohol, she said, "What a pity. You had such good skin."

(736 words)

dribbled: flowed out in small quantities

Source: Stanfield, Sarah. "I Wanted a Tan, but I Wound Up in a Hospital." *Salon*. Salon Media Group, 20 Mar. 2011. Web.

COMPREHENSION

Write an English definition for each word. Try using context clues, or consult a dictionary if necessary. The paragraph number is indicated in parentheses, and in the essay, the words appear in green.

EXAMPLE: balmy (1): ___warm___

1. temper (2): _____
2. sallow (3): _____
3. widespread (4): _____
4. blisters (6): _____
5. sting (6): _____
6. tears (9): _____
7. wounds (9): _____
8. swear (9): _____

Answer the following questions.

9. The essay is called "My Botched Tan." In paragraph 7, the writer refers to the nurse's *botched bleach job*. Guess what the word *botched* means.
_____

10. According to the writer, how do some people in Ecuador feel about their appearance? Give examples from the text.
_____
_____
_____

11. How does the writer feel about her own appearance? Give examples from the text.

_____
_____
_____

12. What did the writer realize after this experience? The answer does not appear in the essay. You need to make a guess and "read between the lines."

_____
_____
_____

 Answer additional reading and listening questions. You can also access audio and video clips online.

WRITING

Write ten questions that you would like to ask the author. Use the present and past tenses.

SPEAKING

Pleasure

Work with a partner and complete the following tasks.
- Add the missing word (*do, does, is, are, did, was,* or *were*) in each question.
- Write your partner's answers in the spaces provided. You can write words or phrases.

Partner's name: _____

1. In the past, what funny movies ___did___ you see? (List two or three movies.)

   Answer: _____
   _____

2. Think about the world's funniest movie. What ___is___ the movie about? In one or two sentences, describe the story.

   Answer: _____
   _____
   _____

3. Who ___is___ your favourite comedian? (A comedian is a performer who makes people laugh.)

   Answer: _____

4. Which activities ___do___ you love to do? Number your top three in order of preference.

   _____ spend time outdoors in nature (walking, taking photos, and so on)

   _____ have a hot soaking bath

   _____ do an exciting sport (skiing, snowboarding, skateboarding, cycling)

   _____ go to a bar with friends and drink

   _____ go online to check Facebook or play games

   _____ (other) _____

CHAPTER 2 | The Pleasure Principle | 27

5. What enjoyable activity ____did____ you do in the past year?

Who ____were____ you with when you did the activity?

Answer _____

_____

_____

_____

WRITING

Write about your partner. Describe his or her preferences and experiences.

READING 2.2

Do you hate those long winter months? Josh Freed tours Russia and discovers that winter can be appreciated. As you read, notice the words in green and guess their meanings.

Winter Love

BY JOSH FREED

1. Last week, while you were freezing in Montreal, I was 7,000 kilometres away, freezing somewhere just as cold. But unlike you, I went shopping at outdoor markets, dining at outdoor barbecues and dancing in the park. I was in Russia, making a documentary film about life in winter nations—and I learned Russians have a very different attitude to winter than we do. Here in 21st-century Canada, we often avoid winter in our heated cars, malls and hockey rinks, though we do go weekend skiing when it's not too cold, or icy, or wet. But for Russians, there's "snow excuse" to stay indoors.

2. My first day there was January 18, their Epiphany, when hundreds of thousands of Russians celebrate by breaking open the winter ice and going for a swim. It was one of the strangest mass events I had ever seen. From midnight to 5 a.m., I joined ten thousand people at a remote lake on a minus 20 Celsius night, where I **shivered** in my Canadian parka and long johns. But hordes of Russian men and women of all ages cheerfully **stripped** to their bathing suits, then **plunged** like penguins into large ice holes—swimming, **dunking**, and **splashing** each other merrily before walking barefoot to their distant cars to down an icy vodka.

3. Many veterans swam long casual laps in larger ice pools, while even Moscow's mayor and Russia's president reportedly did their own icy swims. I did **dip** in a cowardly foot, which came out like a Popsicle, but many who **leaped** in claimed it was exhilarating. Some believe the ice water has healing powers for everything from acne to the common cold. But most just think it's good for the spirit and toughens them up for winter. "We Russians are a stoic people," said one seventy-year-old swimmer. "This is how we face down winter and say, 'I'm stronger than you! I will not change my life by hiding indoors. You can't defeat me winter, try as you might.'"

4. It's typical of Russians' embrace of winter. Many Canadians complain regularly about the cold or simply escape south. But the streets of Moscow and St. Petersburg are always crowded, no matter what the weather. Outdoor markets are open in minus 20 Celsius temperatures, with locals selling books, street

paintings, and fish that's naturally frozen. Ice cream stalls are common because Russians love eating it all winter. They claim it warms them up.

5 Most Russians **strut** the street in elegant fur coats with little interest in the animal rights movement. Explained one Moscow-based journalist: "Russians will never give up their furs. They wear them with pride and panache—refusing to sacrifice style just because it's cold. It's another way they defy winter and laugh in its face."

6 To overcome winter, Russians attack snow with zeal. Moscow gets slightly less snow than Montreal and temperatures that dip to minus 40 Celsius, but the city is cleared almost instantly after a blizzard. Montreal's sophisticated modern snow machinery has nothing over Moscow's rusty old plows and 30,000 workers, mainly women, out day and night who **shovel** piles of snow with wooden shovels in an eternal cold war on snow. Everywhere, you hear the sound of shovelling, as the hammer and sickle are replaced by the hammer and shovel.

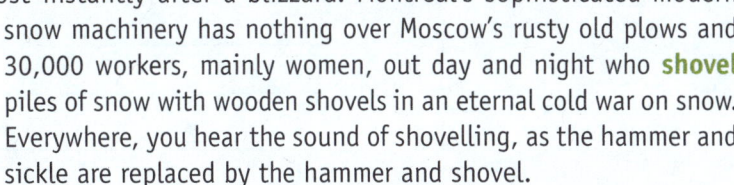

7 My biggest thrill was visiting a large park one snowy Sunday where several hundred Russians, aged fifty to ninety, were outside in their fur coats at their twice-a-week dance party. They did everything from tangos to Beatle tunes, arms raised to the sky to welcome the falling snow. "Why dance indoors when it is so beautiful outside in winter?" asked one woman in her mid-seventies, jitterbugging with a fur-coated gentleman. "You must dance through the cold to warm the soul."

8 I even went to a winter barbecue in the snowy garden of a friend's country dacha one chilly night. A dozen of us barbecued shish kebabs and **downed** chilled vodka in our winter coats. We raised our glasses and toasted to "this beautiful snowy evening, here in nature." I couldn't help wonder why we Canadians don't have winter barbecues. Why don't we dance our way through winter, eating ice cream, instead of hiding indoors? Some say Russians are just tougher people and live as we did decades ago. Others say that Russians have a deeper Nordic winter soul.

9 As a noted Russian novelist told me, "Russians are patriotic about winter. We beat Napoleon and Hitler using winter to freeze the enemy, so we see winter as our ally and friend. To complain about winter is practically to be an enemy of the country," he laughed. "So we celebrate it instead. For us, winter is heaven and the snow is the clouds beneath our feet." Now that's so inspiring I think I'll have an ice cream, then go for a swim in the St. Lawrence.

(819 words)

Source: Freed, Josh. "Russians Greet Winter Like a Long-Lost Friend." *The [Montreal] Gazette*. 29 Jan. 2011. Print.

COMPREHENSION

1 In paragraph 4, what does *embrace* mean?
   a. to hold in your arms
   b. to kiss
   c. to welcome with enthusiasm

2 Who is the essay about? _____

3 Why did Josh Freed go to Russia? _____

4. How do Russians view winter? _____

5. How is winter different in Russia? List at least four ways.
_____
_____
_____
_____

6. What is this essay's main idea? Express the controlling or principal idea in one or two sentences.
_____
_____
_____

WRITING

Write a paragraph explaining why you love or hate a particular season.

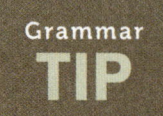

Adjectives

Adjectives modify or provide information about nouns. Sometimes nouns act like adjectives. Remember that adjectives are always singular.

    He loves to be **outdoors**.   He skates in different **outdoor** arenas.

To learn more about plurals and adjectives, see Units 1 and 9 in *Avenues 2: English Grammar*.

Act It Out

The verbs listed below appear in the essay, "Winter Love." Half the class will define the verbs in column A, and the other half will define the verbs in column B.

- Working with a partner, define the verbs in your column using context clues and a dictionary. (The paragraph numbers are indicated in parentheses.)
- Then act out your verbs for a pair of students who worked on the other column. Don't tell them what the verb means; show them. Those students must guess which verbs correspond to your actions.

A	B
shiver (2): _____	dip (3): _____
strip (2): _____	leap (3): _____
plunge (2): _____	strut (5): _____
dunk (2): _____	shovel (6): _____
splash (2): _____	down (8): _____

SPEAKING — Strong Emotions

Work with a partner and write the correct word under each image. Use each word once.

You can use a dictionary, if necessary.

| ashamed | ~~disappointed~~ | ~~embarrassed~~ | ~~relieved~~ | ~~scared~~ |
| ~~deceived~~ | ~~disgusted~~ | lonely | ~~proud~~ | smug |

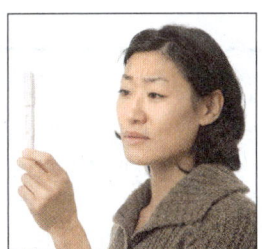

1. Keiko is _disappointed_ because she is not pregnant. She really wants a child.

2. Eric feels _embarrassed_ and _ashamed_ because he forgot his girlfriend's name.

3. Juan is _relieved_ because he passed his law exams.

4. Some older people feel _lonely_ because nobody visits them.

5. Maria is _scared_ because someone just grabbed her from behind.

6. Rachel's husband feels _deceived_. She lied and cheated on him.

7. Alexa is _disgusted_ because she sees a spider in her drink.

8. Mr. Watts feels _proud_ and _smug_ because he just got promoted.

CHAPTER 2 | The Pleasure Principle | 31

Visit the Companion Website to practise using emotions vocabulary.

WRITING

In a paragraph, describe a time in the past when you felt one of the emotions listed on the previous page. Explain what happened.

READING 2.3

Can a good mood be created? Read about a happiness theory.

Act Happy

BY ALBERT NERENBERG

1. We usually think about acting as the preserve of movie stars and annoying people with fake moustaches and bad accents. But a surging scientific theory says acting could make people happy. The Act Happy theory is that we get happier simply by going through the motions of contentment and joy. The theory arises from a controversial concept, sometimes called the body-mind principle, that emotions can be reverse engineered. It's simple: If we feel good, we may smile. But the surprising part is if we smile, we may feel good.

2. Although the Act Happy idea has been bouncing around for years, all of a sudden there's heat around it. There is increasing evidence that the opposite is true—acting enraged, obsessed, malevolent, or depressed may be bad for you. Actor Leonardo DiCaprio developed obsessive-compulsive disorder while playing Howard Hughes in the blockbuster *The Aviator*. In real life, Hughes had the disorder. Actor David Duchovny, who played a writer obsessed with sex in the TV series *Californication*, just checked into a sex-addiction clinic. Batman star Christian Bale allegedly assaulted his mother and sister after completing the violent and brooding *Dark Knight*. Heath Ledger played a tragic and maniacal Joker. Ledger, who had everything going for him, was allegedly clinically depressed. So if people can cultivate rage, depression, and death, can they cultivate joy, hilarity, love, and vitality? If the simple human smile is anything to go by, the answer is yes.

3. Smiling as exercise is both an ancient ritual and a cutting-edge one. A traditional Buddhist adage recommends smiling as the first conscious thing to do each day. Science may concur. Lee Berk, Associate Director of the Centre for Neuroimmunology at Loma Linda University California, was the first to demonstrate that "**mirthful** emotions" or "mirthful laughter" seem to increase the number of T cells, or immune cells, in the bloodstream.

mirthful: joyful

4. Robert Kall is a Philadelphia-based Positive Psychology conference organizer. While working as a therapist, he tried simple smiling as a way to treat depression. "I would put surface electrodes on the smile muscles in people's faces and, using electromyography, would measure the strength of their smiles," he said. "People who were not depressed had smile muscles that were on average four times stronger than people who were depressed," he said. This amazed him. So he began developing what could only be described as a smiling exercise program. "I would have depressed people pump 'smile' iron," he said. "I would have them do repetitions: three sets of twelve every day." By naturally triggering smiles, the "smilercizers" would seem to drive themselves to happier states.

5. Kall warned people not to look at their reflections. "People are generally so self-critical that if they did the exercise in the mirror, they would focus on their perceived flaws rather than smile," he said. But people had positive feelings after their smiling exercises. And in some cases, patients reported that their depression

lifted as a result of the exercise. Kall came out of the experience feeling there was a vast unexplored world out there.

6 There is a good reason why people resist the Act Happy concept. In primordial situations, fake and phony emotions might suggest a trap or danger. We're naturally suspicious around fake smiles, and forced laughter suggests fraud. We gauge our trust in others by their smiles. A put-on smile may suggest dishonesty and therefore danger, and phony laughter may signal manipulation. However, when using emotions to drive positive states, the dishonesty may not matter.

7 Smiling exercises might have been unintentionally applied in charm and etiquette schools. A quick poll finds many of these disciplinarian outfits formally include smile work. "We practise smiling over and over again," says Indiana-based Etiquette School owner Robin Thompson and author of *Be the Best You Can Be*. When asked whether she notices an improvement in the kids' moods when they practise smiling, she replied, "Absolutely, they're more up and perky." Tanisha Wright, who runs the Beautiful Beginnings Charm School in New Jersey, said her students would sometimes burst out laughing while exercising their smile.

8 According to Dr. Mark Stibich, a behaviour change expert at the University of California, San Diego, smiling not only boosts the immune system and lowers blood pressure, it enhances other people's view of you. The weird thing about practising positive emotion is that it makes others more apt to reciprocate. This outcome may be smiling's greatest benefit—connection with others. The Act Happy theory is still at the margins of formal science, but people are starting to run with it, probably because it seems to work. In practice, the fear of phony emotion dissipates quickly and people find they smile and laugh more because they've become good at it.

9 Although it is often viewed with suspicion, acting may just represent a way to expand our emotional range. Acting comes naturally. Kids do it all the time. Since most people can learn to act, perhaps most could learn to Act Happy. If Heath Ledger's tragic torn smile has taught us anything, it may be that we are what we act. So we should be good to ourselves and not forget to smile.

(862 words)

Source: Nerenberg, Albert. "Don't Worry, Act Happy." *The [Montreal] Gazette*. Postmedia Network, 4 Oct. 2010. Web.

VOCABULARY

Highlight ten difficult words in the essay. On a separate sheet of paper, define the words.

COMPREHENSION

For questions 1 to 5, determine if the sentences are true or false. Circle T for "true" or F for "false." If the sentence is false, write a true statement under it.

1. David Duchovny developed obsessive-compulsive disorder after he played Howard Hughes in a movie.   T   F

_____

2. Laughing increases the amount of immune cells in your system.   T   F

_____

3. Robert Kall suggests that people practise smiling in front of a mirror.   T   F

_____

4. People are naturally suspicious of fake smiles.   T   F

_____

5. Tanisha Wright is the author of the book *Be the Best You Can Be*.   T   F

_____

6. According to Dr. Robert Kall, how often should depressed people practise smiling?

_____

7. What is the main or principal idea of the essay?

_____

8. The writer mentions etiquette schools in paragraph 7. How does that support his main point?
   a. Etiquette schools have lots of depressed children.
   b. Etiquette schools prescribe smiling exercises, which make students feel more positive.
   c. Everybody should spend time at an etiquette school.

9. What are the main benefits of smiling? Think of at least two answers.

_____

Humour

Fun means "pleasant" or "a pleasant time."
Funny means "humorous."

My trip to the beach was **fun**. We had a **fun** day. Kayan is so **funny**. He makes me laugh.

Humour (n.) means "the quality of being funny."
Mood means "a temporary state of mind."
Moody means "expressing changeable moods; temperamental."

Michael has a good sense of **humour**. He is always in a good **mood**. He is rarely **moody**.

PRACTICE

Fill in the blanks with *fun*, *funny*, *humour*, *mood*, or *moody*.

1. We are renting a cabin from the Reeds. Mr. Reed looks unhappy. Why is he often in a bad _____? One moment he is friendly, and then the next moment he is angry. He is a very _____ person. We do not have _____ with Mr. Reed.

2. Mrs. Reed, on the other hand, is always friendly. She makes us all laugh. Often, she tells _____ jokes. She does crazy things and is so _____ that we roll on the floor laughing. She has a wonderful sense of _____. When we spend time with her, we always have a lot of _____.

The Greatest Country

What are some advantages and disadvantages of living in the following three countries? Work with a partner or a team of students to fill in the chart.

	Canada	United States	Mexico
Advantages			
Disadvantages			

WRITING

Write about one of the countries listed above. Describe the advantages and disadvantages of living in that country.

Living in Denmark

When you imagine the happiest place on Earth, you might pick a spot with warm sand and soft breezes, a Mediterranean village, perhaps. Learn about the happiest place on Earth. Watch the video and answer the questions.

COMPREHENSION

1. Which country ranked much higher on the "happiness" scale?
   a. Iceland
   b. Fiji

2. What is the main complaint of most people in Denmark?
   _____

3. In Denmark, what is the concept of *yentala*?
   a. Everyone must pay taxes.
   b. Happiness is life's most important goal.
   c. One person is not better than another—people are equal no matter what job they do.

4. What does Jan do for a living?
   _____

Waterfront in Copenhagen, Denmark

CHAPTER 2 | The Pleasure Principle | 35

5 Why does Jan do that job?

_____

_____

6 a) Who is Josef? _____

b) What job does Josef do? _____

7 Describe the Danish concept of *hooga*.

_____

_____

8 Why are people in Denmark so happy? List at least three reasons.

_____

_____

_____

_____

_____

WRITING

With a small group of classmates, create five questions for a happiness survey. Then question your family members and friends. Write about your results.

Take Action!

WRITING TOPICS

Write about one of the following topics. For information about paragraph and essay structure, see the Writing Workshops on pages 137 to 148. Before handing in your work, refer to the Writing Checklist on the inside back cover.

1 A Pleasurable Memory

Choose a photograph that captures a pleasurable moment from your past. Describe what was happening when the picture was taken. Use descriptive words and phrases.

2 Surviving

Write about how to survive a difficult situation. For example, explain how to deal with divorce or a breakup. What are two or three things that people should do to help themselves get through the difficult time?

3 Strategies for Living Well

Write an essay about the good life. In your introduction, you can define what a good life is. Provide two or three supporting ideas. Give specific examples of past experiences from your life and from the lives of people you know.

4 Beauty Ideals

In "The Botched Tan," the writer describes her attempt to change the colour of her skin. How do people try to change their bodies or their fashions to fit beauty ideals? Write about two common ways and give examples from your life and/or the media. For example, consider surgery, dieting, tattoos, piercings, hairstyles, hair colours, and clothing.

SPEAKING TOPICS

Prepare a presentation about one of the following topics.

1. Gratitude Video

Create a video or PowerPoint presentation about the things in life that you are grateful for. To plan for your presentation, create a gratitude journal. Take time to consider what is really worthwhile in your life. Explain why each person, event, or item is important to you.

2. An Awesome Time

Describe an awesome time in your life. You can describe a period of time, a particular event, or a single moment. Where were you? Who were you with? What happened? Why was it awesome?

Visit the Companion Website to listen to a description of a life-changing experience.

3. A Positive Experience

Prepare a presentation about a positive experience that changed your life. If you have trouble coming up with ideas, ask yourself the following questions:

In the past, did I

- overcome any obstacles?
- help or defend someone?
- win or acquire something that I now treasure?
- meet someone who has changed me in a positive way?
- make a really good decision?
- learn a lesson from the experience of a family member or friend?

Explain what happened. Show how the experience helped you or changed you for the better.

4. Act of Kindness Challenge

We live in a period of cynicism, and many people's lives are filled with stress. Give yourself a positive challenge. Do five acts of kindness today. The acts do not have to cost you any money. For example, you can help someone carry groceries, pat someone on the back, give someone a drive home, or give up your seat in a crowded cafeteria to someone who needs it.

First, brainstorm examples of acts of kindness that you could do. Then go and do five of them. In an oral presentation, explain what your acts of kindness were. Where were you, and what happened? Discuss the results of your challenge.

■ VOCABULARY REVIEW

Review key terms from this chapter. Identify any words that you do not understand and learn their meanings.

- ☐ ashamed
- ☐ awesome
- ☐ blisters
- ☐ fun/funny
- ☐ hide
- ☐ mood/moody
- ☐ shiver
- ☐ shovel (n. and v.)
- ☐ smug
- ☐ splash
- ☐ sting
- ☐ wound

To practise vocabulary from this chapter, visit the Companion Website.

SPEAKING PRESENTATION TIPS

- **PRACTISE YOUR PRESENTATION** and time yourself. You should speak for about three minutes or for a length determined by your teacher.
- **USE CUE CARDS.** Do not read! Put a maximum of fifteen words on your cue cards.
- **BRING VISUAL SUPPORT** such as an object, drawing, poster, photograph, or PowerPoint presentation, or create a short video.
- **CLASSMATES WILL ASK YOU QUESTIONS** about your presentation. You must also ask classmates about their presentations. Review how to form questions before your presentation day.

Revising and Editing

REVISE FOR SUPPORTING DETAILS

A good paragraph should include supporting details. Read the paragraph, and add specific examples to make the paragraph more complete. (For more information about paragraph structure, see Writing Workshop 1 on page 137.)

Living in Canada has many advantages. First, there are many beautiful places to visit here. _____

_____

_____

Also, our country has social programs that help average citizens. _____

_____

_____

_____

We should appreciate the advantages of living in our nation.

EDIT FOR NOUNS AND DETERMINERS

Underline and correct eight errors, not including the example. Look for errors with nouns or with *this*, *that*, *these*, or *those*.

          lives
Our lifes have many ordinary awesomes moments. For example, one day last summer, I was home alone. This day, there was a big storm. I heard much loud sounds in the distance. Then, one of the tree on my street fell on an electric wire, and suddenly there was no electricities. I couldn't get informations about the storm because the TV and computer didn't work. Bored, I went to the window and looked outside. All of the persons were inside their dark homes. Suddenly, there was a big flash of lightening. It made everything bright and magical. It reminded me to appreciate each moments. It was awesome.

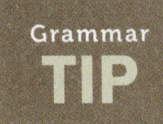

Plural Forms

Always use a plural noun after *one of the*. Use a singular noun after *each* and *every*.

                            lessons   day
One of the most important lesson you can learn is to appreciate each days.

To learn more about nouns, articles, and determiners, see Unit 1 in *Avenues 2: English Grammar*.

"Creativity is allowing yourself to make mistakes. Art is knowing which ones to keep."

– SCOTT ADAMS, CARTOONIST

CHAPTER 3

The Artistic Life

What place do art, literature, and music have in your life? In this chapter, you will read about the artistic life.

40	**START UP** Arts Quiz
42	**LISTENING** Lady Gaga: Poser or Pioneer?
43	**READING 3.1** Interview with Melissa Auf der Maur
46	**READING 3.2** Interview with Jay Baruchel
49	**SPEAKING** The Name Game
50	**WATCHING** TV, Afghanistan Style
52	**READING 3.3** Art and Plagiarism: Does Originality Matter?
55	**SPEAKING** Arts Survey
56	**TAKE ACTION!**
57	**REVISING AND EDITING**

START UP

Arts Quiz

A cultural icon symbolizes a belief or a way of life. Each country has its own cultural icons, and such icons become part of that country's history. Work with a team of students. Look at the clues and then guess the name of each icon.

1. This British author wrote a series of children's books about a boy wizard and his friends. She is now one of England's wealthiest women. _J.K. Rowling_

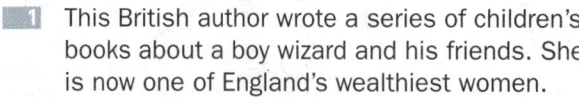

2. This waterfall in Southern Ontario attracts visitors from around the world. It is one of Canada's best known natural attractions. _Niagara Falls_

3. Born in 1984 and raised in Napanee, Ontario, this girl had a recording contract at age sixteen. Her first name means "April." _Avril Lavigne_

4. On April Fool's Day, 1976, these two men created the Apple 1 computer. Give the name of one of the inventors. _Steven Wozniak / Steven Jobs_

5. This man from Liverpool was part of the world's most successful band. Later, he wrote songs asking people to imagine a better world. In 1980, he was murdered by a deranged fan in front of his New York apartment. _John Lennon_

6. This metal tower was built for the 1889 World's Fair in Paris. It sits on the Champ de Mars. _Eiffel Tower_

7. This actress from London, Ontario, had her first role as the Queen Bee in *Mean Girls*. She went on to act in *The Notebook* and *Sherlock Holmes*. _Rachel McAdams_

8. Quebec-born Guy Laliberté was a street performer who mixed spectacular staging with acrobatics to create this world-famous circus. The shows are a top draw in Las Vegas. _Cirque du Soleil_

9. This actor and writer from Vancouver co-wrote *Superbad* and *Pineapple Express*. He had the leading role in *Knocked Up*. _Seth Rogen (?)_

10. This iconic Canadian bird has a black head and neck and flies in "V" formations. _Canada Goose_

11. This Nova Scotia native won a Stanley Cup with the Pittsburgh Penguins in 2009, as well as a gold medal for Canada in the 2010 Vancouver Winter Olympics. _Sidney Crosby_

12. This Montreal-based indie-rock band won awards for its album *The Suburbs*. The band includes husband and wife duo Win Butler and Régine Chassagne. The Band's name is hot. _Arcade Fire_

13. This young man from Stratford, Ontario, had his first success on YouTube. Many boys copied his hairstyle. This young man's fans became known as "beliebers." _Justin Bieber_

14. Born Stefani Germanotta, this pop star gained notoriety for her odd fashion sense and catchy club singles, such as "Born This Way." _Lady Gaga_

15. This former Harvard student created the popular social networking site, Facebook. _Mark Zuckerberg_

LISTENING PRACTICE

1. Pronounce Past Tense Verbs

Regular past tense verbs end in *-ed*. Review pronunciation rules.

Pronunciation TIP

REGULAR PAST TENSE VERBS

RULE	SOUND	EXAMPLES
When the verb ends in *s, k, f, x, ch,* or *sh*, the final *-ed* is pronounced *t*.	t	asked wished
When the verb ends in *t* or *d*, the final *-ed* is pronounced as a separate syllable.	id	added wanted
In all other regular verbs, the final *-ed* is pronounced *d*.	d	lived moved

Say each verb twice. Then indicate if the verb ends with a *t, d,* or *id* sound.

EXAMPLE: added   t   d   (id)

1. pushed   (t) d id
2. planted   t   d (id)
3. discussed (t) d id
4. opened   t   (d) id
5. divided   t   d (id)
6. missed   (t) d id
7. sounded   t   d (id)
8. wished   (t) d id
9. tried   t   (d) id
10. pointed t   d (id)

2. Pronounce Sentences and Identify Verbs

Pronounce each sentence after the speaker. Then write the missing verbs.

Pronunciation TIP

IRREGULAR PAST TENSE VERBS

RULE	SOUND	EXAMPLES
When the verb ends in *–ought* or *–aught*, pronounce the final letters as *ot*.	ot	bought taught caught

1. Picasso ___started___ to paint when he was a child.
2. His father ___bought___ a lot of art supplies.
3. The boy ___decided___ to study in an art school.
4. An older artist ___taught___ him a lot about art.
5. They ___discussed___ art, and the boy ___asked___ many questions.
6. They ___walked___ outside, and they ___talked___ for hours.
7. Sometimes they ___fought___ about an idea.
8. At his first show, he ___counted___ thirty people in the gallery.
9. Many people ___thought___ that Picasso's art was unusual.
10. I ___brought___ a sculpture home, and I ___placed___ it on a shelf.

Practise your spelling by doing dictations.

LISTENING — Lady Gaga: Poser or Pioneer?

Is Lady Gaga just a copy of Madonna? Is she a poser, or is she a unique and original artist? In an interview with Jian Ghomeshi, Kate Durbin defends Gaga.

LISTENING FOR DETAILS

1. What is the name of Kate Durbin's online journal? _____

2. According to Durbin, why should Lady Gaga be an academic topic?
   a. She "performs" fame to highlight it and make a comment on it.
   b. She is a better singer and performer than Madonna.
   c. She writes songs with profound meanings that are like poetry.

3. Which singer is Lady Gaga most often compared to? _____

4. According to Durbin, how does Lady Gaga approach older pop stars?
   a. She mimics them in an effort to show how stupid fame is.
   b. She is respectful. She borrows from her elders but takes it to another level.

5. What is M.I.A.'s opinion of Lady Gaga?
   a. Mainly positive   b. Mainly negative

6. According to Kate Durbin, how is Lady Gaga really different from Madonna? List at least two ways.

   _____
   _____
   _____

7. Durbin argues that Lady Gaga is not a rip-off artist. What is a rip-off artist?
   a. A woman who removes her clothing in public.
   b. A person who has a very violent artistic image.
   c. A person who steals ideas from others.

LISTENING FOR THE MAIN IDEA

8. What is Kate Durbin's main point about Lady Gaga?

   _____
   _____

DISCUSSION AND WRITING

1. What famous person living today will probably still be famous in one hundred years? Explain why that person will still be famous.

2. Imagine that you can interview any actor, artist, or musician who is alive today. Compose ten questions for that person on a separate piece of paper.

Question Forms

In questions, generally put the auxiliary before the subject.

Art has a purpose.	**Does** art have a purpose?
He took piano lessons.	**Did** he take piano lessons?

Exception: When the main verb is *be*, just move *be* before the subject.

He was famous.	**Was** he famous?

To learn more about question forms, see Units 2 to 6 in *Avenues 2: English Grammar*.

42 | PART 1 | The Good Life

READING 3.1

Read about the experiences of a Canadian bass player.

PAIR READING ACTIVITY (OPTIONAL)

Work with a partner and read either Reading 3.1 or 3.2. Then answer the questions that follow your reading. Later, you will share information with your partner (see page 48).

Interview with Melissa Auf der Maur

1. Melissa Auf der Maur was born and raised in Montreal. In mid-1994, she was invited to join Courtney Love's band Hole after Hole's bass player, Kristen Pfaff, died of a drug overdose. From 1994 to 1999, Melissa was the bass player for Love's band. In an interview with Ben Kaplan of the *National Post*, Melissa said, "When I first took a plane to Seattle, there was Courtney Love at the baggage claim. Not only had she just lost her husband [Kurt Cobain], but I was replacing a deceased woman in her band. I knew what I was doing was far bigger than music. It was more about a life's destiny."

2. When Melissa's five-year contract with Hole expired, she was planning to create her own music when she received a phone call from Billy Corgan of the Smashing Pumpkins. Melissa joined the Pumpkins for a farewell tour. After her stint with the Pumpkins, Melissa devoted herself to her own projects. *Avenues* asked Melissa some questions.

3. **Why did you decide to learn the bass?**

FACE: Fine Arts Core Education, a Montreal school that emphasizes the arts.

4. I went to art school as a child in Montreal. At the school, **FACE**, I played the trumpet and sang in choirs, so my ear and understanding of music developed early in life. But the real way I learned to play rock music and bass was by listening to music constantly and spending all my time with people who love and play music. I was a DJ at a small bar for six years. I eventually started to play music with other local musicians on my nights off. Pretty much every night revolved around music in my youth—and that is still true today.

5. **How did you meet Billy Corgan of the Smashing Pumpkins?**

6. As an avid new music follower, I went to as many shows as I could when I was young. The early 1990s was a very exciting time in music. Foufounes Électriques, Montreal's legendary punk rock club, booked all the new bands from the USA. There were "Loonie Tuesdays" where you could pay $1 to see a new band. That's where I saw the Smashing Pumpkins play their first ever Montreal gig on their first full North American tour. There were about thirty people in the club, and the band played with such intensity and force. Instantly, I was converted to a fan for life. I had rarely seen such grandiosity and dramatics in such a small club before.

brawl: fight

7. My friend Bruce was with me. The very thing that attracted me, he thought was too much attitude. So in protest, Bruce threw a beer bottle at Billy Corgan between songs. A little **brawl** started between the two of them. The bouncers broke it up. Instead of ending the show, Billy got back up on stage and said "Montreal, we have one more for you." They played "I Am One," which was the first track of their first album. That is still my favourite Pumpkins song.

8 As they were loading their gear off stage, I went and introduced myself to Billy. I apologized on behalf of Montreal. I told him I loved the music and would follow it from then on. We became pen pals.

9 **How did that meeting change your life?**

10 First and foremost, the music itself changed my life. It gave me a vision of what I wanted to do with my life. The sound of the music was so powerful and so familiar, as if I had found a part of my future self. The instant friendship with Billy changed my life on a practical level. When they returned three years later to promote their second album, *Siamese Dream*, my first band, Tinker, got to open for them at the Metropolis. That put our name on the musical map locally. And Billy saw me play. That led him to recommend me to Courtney Love when Hole needed a new bass player.

Patty Schemel, Courtney Love, and Melissa Auf der Maur

11 **When you started working with Courtney Love, she was a recent widow—her husband Kurt Cobain had died a while earlier. Nirvana was huge at that time, and Courtney Love was in all of the newspapers. What was it like to work with her?**

12 The greatest pride I have in regards to my time and union with Courtney was that we were representing women in a male-dominated landscape. She and I are polar opposites, but we were united in our mission of women in music. It was a very exciting and extreme chapter of my life. It was a life-defining time. I am eternally grateful that Courtney asked me to join her band. I travelled the world and played and performed constantly while representing women. Those were invaluable life lessons.

13 **Your first show with Hole was in front of about 60,000 people at a festival in Reading, England. How did it feel the first time you performed before a huge audience?**

14 It was like a surreal dream that had become my real life. I felt pretty comfortable from the get-go. In fact, it's easier to play to big crowds than to little ones. The details get lost in the big shows.

15 **After you left Hole, you joined the Smashing Pumpkins. What were some differences between working with Hole and with the Pumpkins?**

16 Hole gave me lessons in life. The Smashing Pumpkins gave me lessons in music.

17 **What are you working on now?**

18 Although I've been playing music for over a decade, I am still an artist in development as far as my own projects are concerned. I recently released my second solo album, *Out of Our Minds*. It's an album with an extended fantasy film and comic book element, so I was able to join my passion for music with my love of visual and conceptual arts. It's also my first independently produced and released venture. Establishing my own artist-run company has been an important step in my artistic life. The rise of technology and changes in the music industry both present a great opportunity for artists to take matters in their own hands.

19 **What advice would you give college students who want to be in the arts?**

20 Work hard and follow your heart. Do what you love and be yourself. Be honest and generous. That's really all you need.

(1062 words)

VOCABULARY AND COMPREHENSION

1. In paragraph 6, Melissa calls herself "an avid new music follower." Guess the meaning of *avid* by looking at the context.
   a. new
   b. enthusiastic
   c. lost

2. What three bands did Melissa Auf der Maur work with?
   _____ _____ _____

3. Who is Courtney Love? _____
   _____

4. In paragraph 11, Courtney Love is called "a recent widow." What is a widow?
   a. a woman whose husband died
   b. a singer who is very successful
   c. a person who is very sad

5. How did Melissa meet Billy Corgan? Describe what happened.
   _____
   _____
   _____

6. How did Melissa's first meeting with Billy Corgan change her life? List at least two ways.
   _____
   _____
   _____
   _____
   _____

7. Why is it easier to play music before a large audience than before a small one?
   _____

8. How is Melissa's newest album different from her previous work?
   a. She plays a different style of music.
   b. She changed to a new record company.
   c. She produced and released it herself.

GRAMMAR LINK

9. Underline six irregular past tense verbs in paragraph 7. Then, in the chart, write the past form and the base form of the verbs.

	Past Form	Base Form
1.	was	be
2.	_____	_____
3.	_____	_____
4.	_____	_____
5.	_____	_____
6.	_____	_____

10. The first sentence of paragraph 8 is the following: "As they **were loading** their gear off stage, I went and introduced myself to Billy." Why is the first verb in the past progressive tense?
    _____

Answer additional reading and listening questions. You can also access audio and video clips online.

READING 3.2 — What is life like for a professional actor? Read an interview with Canadian actor Jay Baruchel.

Interview with Jay Baruchel

BY JASPER ANSON

1 What do Clint Eastwood, Robert Downey Jr., and Nicolas Cage have in common? They are all stops on the professional résumé of the forever earnest Canadian actor Jay Baruchel. Born in Ottawa, Ontario, in 1982 [and raised in Montreal], he started in the acting world by guest-starring on a number of Canadian television series in the mid-1990s. After an early television gig with an unknown Elisha Cuthbert as co-hosts of Canada's *Popular Mechanics for Kids*, he cracked the Hollywood circuit with a small role in Cameron Crowe's rock opus *Almost Famous*. From there, Judd Apatow cast him in a lead role in the critically-acclaimed 2001 TV series, *Undeclared*. Though the series did not pull in the expected **ratings**, Jay Baruchel got a cult following out of the deal as well as a valuable industry ally.

ratings: percentage of viewers

2 Before working with Judd Apatow again in 2007's *Knocked Up*, Jay Baruchel would join the cast of Clint Eastwood's Oscar-winning 2004 effort, *Million Dollar Baby*, to play the impossibly optimistic young boxer Danger Barch. As he continues to impress many with his everyman qualities, Jay Baruchel is becoming equally in demand on both sides of the border, thanks to roles in Hollywood fare (*Tropic Thunder*, *She's Out of My League*, *The Sorcerer's Apprentice*) and homegrown Canadian movies like 2010's *The Trotsky*. AskMen caught up with Jay Baruchel.

Jay Baruchel in *Knocked Up*

utmost: greatest

3 **You have alternated a lot between Hollywood films and smaller Canadian movies. As a Canadian actor, how important is it for you to make time for projects back home?**

4 It is of the **utmost** importance to me, man. I have a maple leaf tattoo over my heart, quite literally, and my two favourite things on earth are being in Canada and making movies. If it were up to me, every job I get would be in Montreal. I feel an obligation to use whatever I have going on down south to help people get to see movies up here because this is the greatest country in the world. I think kids here should be proud of their own TV shows and their movies.

5 **From your perspective so far, do you notice any differences between Canadian and American movies?**

greenlit: authorized; given permission to proceed

6 We make fewer movies here, but the movies that get **greenlit** here are purer films. To get a movie made in Los Angeles, you have to [use] notes and thoughts and ideas from a myriad of different people at every step of the process—from the script to production and editing. In Canada, when they greenlight a movie, they like the script. They might let you make the movie, and so it is a purer form of art up here. Also, when there is less money involved, people are less stressed and feel freer to contribute and try things. I've had a lovely career in the States and I've worked with some amazing people and I've made some pretty **badass** flicks, but it is way less stressful making movies up here.

badass: street language meaning "great"

Undeclared: an American television comedy that aired in 2001 and 2002

7 **One of the people who had a major impact on your career is Judd Apatow, who cast you in *Undeclared* with Seth Rogen. How did that role help your career?**

8 I definitely think those seventeen episodes of *Undeclared* are of great importance to a lot of people, and that means a lot to me. That was my coming out party, man. Nobody knew me down there [in the United States] and all of a sudden, there I was. So that role had major value for my career. When I stayed with [Seth Rogen] in LA, we spent a good deal of our time watching that TV show. Judd is just interested in what is happening and what is real. He is brilliant, and he has this great intuition as to what is funny. I remember asking him if he ever wanted to do a drama, and he said, "Why? Life is funny."

9 **Another movie you were in was *Million Dollar Baby* for Clint Eastwood. What stands out for you as your favourite moment on the set with him?**

10 Arguing politics with him was pretty fun. The first day on the set, I was super stressed because he's still, to this day, the only man that I've ever worked for who could impress my granddad. People love *Knocked Up*, but my granddad couldn't have cared less. But Clint is freakin' Clint, man, and for males of many generations, Clint is incredibly important. He is the nicest guy ever.

Jay Baruchel in *Tropic Thunder*

11 **You worked with Nicolas Cage in *The Sorcerer's Apprentice*. Is there anything you want to say about Nicolas Cage?**

12 He is the man. He was incredibly kind to me, and I count him as one of my friends. He's a bona fide artist and he's one of the most professional, kind guys I've ever worked with. I would make him mix CDs and give him comic books and stuff. We're both huge **nerds** and we both just geeked out for six months.

nerds: intelligent people who are obsessed with a hobby

13 **Ben Stiller directed you in *Tropic Thunder* with Robert Downey Jr. and Jack Black. Those actors have a certain creative brand. If somebody is going to say, "I'm going to see the new Jay Baruchel movie," what would you want people to expect from that?**

14 I might not be able to **chew scenery** as well as some guys, and I might not be as interesting standing still or whatever, but I think the one thing that I've got going for me is truth and honesty. I hope that when people go to see me, they feel like I'm a guy that they'd know from parties or a bar or something—like I'm a guy that they know from outside of movies.

chew scenery: act dramatically and enthusiastically

15 **What can you tell us about your future plans?**

16 When I get to make my own movie, it'll be the culmination of my life's work. Long before I ever started acting, I always knew I wanted to be a director. I have always wanted to direct horror movies and scare the s*** out of people.

(1002 words)

Source: Anson, Jasper. "Jay Baruchel Interview." *AskMen*. IGN Entertainment, 2011. Web.

VOCABULARY AND COMPREHENSION

1. Paragraph 1 states that Baruchel "cracked the Hollywood circuit." What does this mean?

    a. People began to know and accept him in Hollywood.

    b. He became addicted to a dangerous drug.

    c. He broke his arm while he was working in Hollywood.

2. Paragraph 1 says that *Undeclared* "did not pull in the expected ratings." What does this mean?
   a. The show had fewer viewers than the network expected.
   b. The show was extremely popular, more than the network expected.

3. Where is Jay from? _____

4. Where is Jay's tattoo of a maple leaf? _____

5. In paragraph 6, Jay refers to "here." Where is here?
   a. The United States   b. Canada

6. In what order were Jay's acting jobs? Number them from 1 (the earliest) to 6 (the most recent).

   _____ *Popular Mechanics for Kids*

   _____ *Million Dollar Baby*

   _____ *Almost Famous*

   _____ *The Trotsky*

   _____ *Undeclared*

   _____ *Knocked Up*

7. How did Judd Apatow impact Jay's career?

   _____
   _____
   _____
   _____

8. How is movie making different in Canada compared to the United States?

   _____
   _____
   _____
   _____

9. What is Jay's main message to Canadians? (See paragraph 4.)

   _____
   _____

GRAMMAR LINK

10. The first sentence in paragraph 9 is: "Another movie you **were** in **was** *Million Dollar Baby* for Clint Eastwood." What are the subjects of the verbs *were* and *was*?

subject	verb	subject	verb
_____	were	_____	was

PAIR READING: SHARE YOUR INFORMATION

Compare Melissa Auf der Maur and Jay Baruchel. Discuss the following points with a partner who read the other text. Write your information in the chart.

	Melissa Auf der Maur	Jay Baruchel
Childhood		
Person who influenced his or her career (explain how)		
Major career highlights		
Current or future project		

WRITING

In artistic careers, talent is important. But what role does luck play? Explain the importance of luck and good timing in an artistic career. As you answer the question, consider the careers of Jay Baruchel and Melissa Auf der Maur.

SPEAKING

The Name Game

In this fast-paced game, you must give clues about famous people. To prepare for the game, do the following:

1. Begin by cutting a paper into five small pieces. On each paper, write the name of a famous person. The person can be famous in the world of music, art, film, sports, or politics, and can be living or dead. Try to choose people from different fields. Fold your papers so the names aren't visible. Give your papers to your teacher.

2. Then form teams of at least five students. Your teacher will shuffle the papers and give a box of names to each team.

3. The oldest student on your team begins. That player pulls a name out of the box and tries to get the student on his or her right to guess who that famous person is. The player can provide clues, but cannot spell or say the actual name. For example, if the famous person is Madonna, the player can say, "She's an American singer, in her fifties, with blond hair. She also makes movies." After the name is guessed correctly, the clue giver keeps that paper. (If the student can't make the guess, the person

speaking gets no points.) Each turn lasts twenty seconds, so he or she can continue pulling names out of the box until the twenty seconds are over. After the first clue giver's turn, the student to his or her right goes next.

The team with the most correct guesses at the end of the game wins.

Note: When it is your turn, be careful not to let anyone see the name that is on your paper. Give clues as quickly as you can. **If you use a word that is not English, your turn instantly ends.**

WATCHING TV, Afghanistan Style

Susan Ormiston visits two Afghan television personalities. Watch the video and answer the following questions.

COMPREHENSION

1. These days, what percentage of Afghans have access to television?
   a. 25 percent   b. 65 percent   c. 80 percent

2. Sami Mahdi has a television show called *Niqab*. What does *Niqab* mean? _____

3. Why does he do programs about women's issues?
   _____
   _____

4. What problems does he have with the live debate shows?
   _____
   _____

5. He did a live political debate about peace with the Taliban. What was the result of the vote?
   a. Two to one voted against peace with the Taliban.
   b. Two to one voted for peace with the Taliban.

6. What types of content are banned on state-run television in Afghanistan?
   _____

7. In what Canadian city did Mozhdah Jamalzadah grow up? _____

8. During a walk in a shopping mall, Jamalzadah saw a photo that worried her. What was the photo for?
   a. her TV show   b. her album cover   c. her movie

9. What types of topics does Jamalzadah cover on her show?
   _____

10. What is Jamalzadah afraid of?
    _____
    _____

Mozhdah Jamalzadah

DISCUSSION AND WRITING

With a partner, prepare eight questions that you would like to ask Sami Mahdi or Mozhdah Jamalzadah. Use at least two verb tenses in your questions.

READING STRATEGY

Thinking Critically

In order to evaluate a text critically, ask yourself the follo[wing]

1. **What is the author's purpose?**
   When you read, consider what the author's purpose [is]. authors write for one of the following reasons:
   - **To inform.** Authors use facts to educate the reader.
   - **To persuade.** Authors use facts and opinions to argue a point. They hope to influence the reader.
   - **To entertain.** Authors hope to get an emotional response from the reader. The text may evoke laughter, tears, anger, frustration, or shock.

2. **Is the text based on fact or opinion?**
   A **fact** is something that can be proven to be true or false. It is based on evidence and on personal observation. An **opinion** is a statement of personal feeling or judgement.

   Fact: Vigorous dance increases the heart rate.
   Opinion: Dance is an enjoyable exercise.

PRACTICE

Read the following paragraphs and answer the questions.

1. Many early hip-hop artists were also disc jockeys. They took excerpts or "samples" from recordings to create the backgrounds for their songs. Sometimes they would repeat or combine samples in a technique called "looping." The artists whose music was sampled viewed this as stealing and sued. Eventually, rap artists started to acknowledge the sources from which they took their samples, and they paid royalties to those sources.

   Barkley, Elizabeth F. *Crossroads*. 2nd Ed. Pearson: Upper Saddle River, 2007. Print.

   1. What is this an example of?   ☐ opinion   ☐ fact
   2. What is the author's purpose?   ☐ to inform   ☐ to persuade   ☐ to entertain
   3. What is the paragraph about? Sum it up in one sentence.
   _____
   _____

2. "Born This Way," by Lady Gaga, sounds just a *weeeeee* bit (read *exactly*) like an '80s pop music mega-hit you may have heard of called "Express Yourself," by Madonna. Yes, the chord progressions are the same. Yes, the dance beat is pretty in sync. Yes, the lyrical content is identical ("Be yourself! / Love yourself!"). That doesn't make it any less brilliant.

   "Lady Gaga's 'Born This Way' Rips Off Madonna's 'Express Yourself.' So What?" *Methodshop*. MethodShop.com, 2011. Web.

   1. What is this an example of?   ☐ opinion   ☐ fact
   2. What is the author's purpose?   ☐ to inform   ☐ to persuade   ☐ to entertain
   3. What is the paragraph about? Sum it up in one sentence.
   _____
   _____
   _____

Prepare for your reading tests by visiting the Companion Website. Click on "Reading Strategies" to find a variety of practice exercises.

READING 3.3

These days, many artists incorporate the work of others into their songs or novels. At what point does a "remix" become plagiarism? Laura Miller considers the case of a young writer.

Art and Plagiarism: Does Originality Matter?

BY LAURA MILLER

uproar: heated controversy

overblown: excessive; disproportionate

boost: increase

1. In 2009, Helene Hegemann, a seventeen-year-old German author, wrote a best-selling tale of drugging and clubbing, *Axolotl Roadkill*. She was accused of plagiarism but defended the practice, telling one German newspaper, "I don't feel it is stealing because I put all the material into a completely different and unique context."

2. In her novel, Hegemann lifted text from an obscure, independently published novel, *Strobo*, by a blogger known as Airen. Another German blogger, Deef Pirmasens, was the first to point out that passages from *Axolotl Roadkill* are duplicated from *Strobo*, with small changes.

3. Despite the **uproar** caused by this revelation, *Axolotl Roadkill* has been selling better than ever. It was also nominated for the $20,000 fiction prize at the Leipzig Book Fair. [It didn't win.] "Obviously, it isn't completely clean but, for me, it doesn't change my appraisal of the text," a jury member and newspaper book critic told *The New York Times*, explaining that the jury knew about the plagiarism accusations when it selected the novel for its short list. "I believe it's part of the concept of the book."

4. "There's no such thing as originality anyway, just authenticity," Hegemann pronounced in a statement to the press. To this conundrum, Hegemann has added a heaping dollop of generational special pleading. The story has prompted teachers to offer multiple examples of students who don't seem to understand what plagiarism is or that it's wrong. Kids these days, this line of reasoning goes, have unfathomably different values, and their elders had better come to terms with this.

5. Count me among those who think that most plagiarism scandals are **overblown**. A classic example is the novelist Ian McEwan, who replicated in *Atonement* a few phrases from a memoir he used as historical research for that novel. What smells off in this instance is precisely Hegemann's claim to be using her borrowings to advance a cutting-edge concept of artistry. The daughter of an avant-garde dramatist, Hegemann says she practises "intertextuality" and explains, "Many artists use this technique. By organically including parts in my text, I am entering into a dialogue with the author." This would be more plausible if Hegemann had acknowledged from the beginning that she had included work from other writers in *Axolotl Roadkill*, but by all indications, she did not. (McEwan *did* credit the out-of-print nurse's memoir he used as a source for *Atonement*.)

6. Some supporters have pointed out that, thanks to *Axolotl Roadkill*, *Strobo* is now enjoying a sales **boost**, proving that "remixes" can be a rising tide that lifts all boats. However, remember that it took another blogger's plagiarism accusation to bring Airen's involuntary "contribution" to *Axolotl Roadkill* to the public's attention. If Hegemann intended to enter into a dialogue with Airen, she took pains to make it look like a monologue. If she viewed the writing itself as collaborative, she suppressed any urge to share those handsome royalty checks.

7 In an interview with the German magazine *Spiegel*, the person Hegemann plagiarized has weighed in. Airen, the blogger, is just under thirty years old. Several years ago, when he first arrived in Berlin, he had a white-collar job, but he spent his evenings in nightclubs. He began blogging about drugs and sex. As he says in the Speigel interview, "It was a combination that spun out of control. The writing fed on the partying, and the partying fed on the writing." Airen "became locked in a vicious circle of excess" as he imbibed a variety of dangerous drugs and had sex with strangers in public toilets.

8 These days, Airen has quit drugs, is married, and works for a respectable company. He is concerned that his work colleagues could find out about his previous exploits. Naturally, he was stunned when he learned that parts of his life story have appeared in a best-selling German novel—written by someone else. *Axolotl* is full of interesting sections," he says. "There was really no need for her to copy me. But she borrowed entire passages of dialogue. I feel like my copyright has been infringed."

9 How innovative is Hegemann's novel? Since both *Axolotl Roadkill* and *Strobo* recount life among the youngest participants in Berlin's wild club scene, Hegemann's claim to be presenting the material in a "completely different and unique context" seems **a stretch**. And—please!—how much longer can very young writers publish novels depicting drug use and casual sex and *still* provoke wonder among their elders? It happens every few years, yet every new version is treated like some shocking, never-before-imagined exposé, when, really, only the playlist changes. The enthusiasm for *Axolotl Roadkill* seems to boil down to titillated astonishment. You can't blame other seventeen-year-olds for finding it incredibly **daring** and fresh, but as for us adults—shouldn't we know better?

(769 words)

a stretch: not credible

daring: courageous; rebellious

Source: Adapted from Miller, Laura. "Plagiarism: The Next Generation." *Salon.com*. Salon Media Group, 16 Feb. 2010. Web.

VOCABULARY AND COMPREHENSION

1 In paragraph 2, what does *lifted* mean? Ensure that you read the word in context before you make your guess.

  a. raised up   b. appropriated   c. helped

2 Paragraph 3 begins with the words "Despite the uproar caused by this revelation …." Which phrase could replace the original phrase, but keep the same meaning?

  a. Because of the uproar …
  b. Instead of the uproar …
  c. Regardless of the uproar …

3 In paragraph 5, the author uses the expression *smells off* to describe Hegemann's claim. What does she mean?

  a. It has an unpleasant odour.
  b. It is doubtful and difficult to believe.
  c. It is old and dirty.

4 What is the title of the book that the blogger Airen published? _____

5 In *Atonement*, Ian McEwan borrowed a few phrases from another text. Did he credit the original author?   ☐ Yes   ☐ No

6. In *Axolotl Roadkill*, Hegemann borrowed passages from the blogger Airen. Did she credit the original author? Explain your answer.
_____
_____

7. Paragraph 7 states that Airen became *locked in a vicious circle of excess*. What does this mean?
   a. He stopped doing drugs.
   b. Doing drugs and having dangerous sexual encounters led to writing about them on his blog, which in turn led to more dangerous drugs and sex.
   c. He became a drug addict.

8. Find a word in paragraph 8 that means "not respected; violated."
_____

9. What is Airen's opinion of the controversy? See paragraph 8.
_____
_____

10. Does the author express her opinion of Hegemann? ☐ Yes ☐ No
    If you answered "yes," explain what her opinion is. Provide proof from a paragraph.
_____
_____

11. What is the author's opinion of "club scene" novels? See paragraph 9.
_____
_____

12. What is the author's purpose? ☐ to inform ☐ to persuade ☐ to entertain
    Explain your answer. _____
_____
_____

WRITING

In paragraph 4, the author writes that students today "don't seem to understand what plagiarism is or that it's wrong." Is that a fair statement? In a paragraph, present your opinion about cheating in schools and colleges. Support your main idea with specific examples.

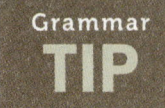

Shifting Point of View

When you write an essay about *students* or *people*, keep the point of view consistent in your general sentences. For example, do not shift unnecessarily from *they* to *you* or *we*.

                                          they
Students often cheat. Sometimes, ~~you~~ copy material from the Internet.

Vocabulary BOOST

Idioms and Expressions

The words or expressions in bold appear in this chapter's readings. The page and paragraph numbers are indicated in parentheses. Match each expression with its meaning.

Expressions	Meanings
1. from the **get-go** (page 44, paragraph 14)	a. a great guy
2. **take matters into their own hands** (page 44, paragraph 18)	b. beginning
3. He **cracked** the Hollywood **circuit**. (page 46, paragraph 1)	c. get a lot of viewers
4. It didn't **pull in the ratings**. (page 46, paragraph 1)	d. take control of a project
5. He is **the man**. (page 47, paragraph 12)	e. not credible
6. to **lift** text (page 52, paragraph 2)	f. can be summed up as
7. My copyright has been **infringed**. (page 53, paragraph 8)	g. appropriate; steal
8. It's **a stretch**. (page 53, paragraph 9)	h. became known and accepted
9. It **boils down to** titillated astonishment. (page 53, paragraph 9)	i. not respected; violated

SPEAKING

Arts Survey

Work with a team of four or five students and prepare an arts survey. Your survey can be about one of the following topics.

| reading | movies | painting | graffiti |
| dance | music | television | video or online games |

Your team should prepare at least six questions about your topic.

EXAMPLES: Do you play a musical instrument?   ☐ Yes   ☐ No

How often do you read comic books?
a. never   b. once a year
c. every month   d. every week

Note: If you ask a knowledge question, give respondents an "I don't know" choice.

EXAMPLES: Who is Drake?
a. a painter   b. a dancer
c. a singer   d. I don't know

After you have completed your questions, number your team members from 1 to 5. Then get together with the students in the other teams who have the same number as you do. For example, all of the 1s will sit together and survey each other. All of the 2s, 3s, 4s, and 5s will do the same thing.

After you finish surveying your new group, return to your original team and compile your answers. Later, you can present your survey results to the class or write about them.

Take Action!

WRITING TOPICS

Write about one of the following topics. For information about paragraph and essay structure, see the Writing Workshops on pages 137 to 148. Before handing in your work, refer to the Writing Checklist on the inside back cover.

1 The Value of Music

Stephen Pinker, a psychology professor at Harvard, argues that music is useless. He says, "It could vanish from our species and the rest of our lifestyle would be virtually unchanged." Write an essay arguing that we need music. Provide two reasons why it is important. Give specific examples of singers and songs. You could discuss the ways that people use music in our society. For example, refer to the reading "Interview with Melissa Auf der Maur."

Note: Place quotation marks around the titles of songs, and put the titles of CDs in italics.
  "Poker Face" was on Lady Gaga's CD *The Fame*.

2 Compare Celebrities

Compare two celebrities mentioned in this chapter. You could discuss any of the following people: Melissa Auf der Maur, Jay Baruchel, Sami Mahdi (from the TV show *Niqab*) or Mozhdah Jamalzadah. Think of at least two ways in which they are similar and/or different. For example, you can compare their political actions, their passions, the role of "luck" in their careers, and so on.

3 Media Influence

Explain how programs created for television or the Internet have a positive and/or negative influence on people. You can provide examples from the video *TV: Afghanistan Style*. You can also discuss other programs that you are familiar with, such as reality programs, talk shows, dramas, and comedies.

4 Role Models

Describe influential people in your life. (Think about people who have influenced your career choice or your artistic tastes. You can also consider those who have influenced you politically or morally.) First, describe one or more people who influenced you in the past. Then describe someone who influences you today.

5 Art and Theft

Most people would never steal a DVD from a store. So why do people download music and movies from illegal websites? Why do some writers and musicians "remix" and borrow content from others? In an essay, discuss art and theft. Explain why people feel comfortable stealing artistic content when it is online. Provide at least two reasons and include specific examples from your life. You can also refer to the essay "Art and Plagiarism: Does Originality Matter?"

SPEAKING TOPICS

Prepare a presentation about one of the following topics.

1 Concert Review

Talk about a time you saw live music. It could be in a club or concert hall. Describe the experience. Begin by describing the singer or band and the concert venue. Approximately when and where was the concert? Who did you go with? Then present your evaluation of the show. Why was it fantastic or terrible? Use details to describe what you saw and heard. End with a prediction about the band.

■ VOCABULARY REVIEW

Review key terms from this chapter. Identify any words that you do not understand and learn their meanings.

- ☐ avid
- ☐ boost
- ☐ brawl
- ☐ director
- ☐ gig
- ☐ nerds
- ☐ overblown
- ☐ ratings
- ☐ script
- ☐ uproar
- ☐ utmost
- ☐ widow

 To practise vocabulary from this chapter, visit the Companion Website.

2 Fame: Advantages and Problems

Discuss the advantages and/or disadvantages of fame. Tell stories about specific celebrities, and explain what happened to them. Then describe who will be famous next year or predict which celebrity will have problems.

3 Music Trends

Discuss a music-related trend from the past. For example, you can describe a boy band, a singer, a music listening device, or a dance. Then describe a current popular trend related to music. Predict a future trend.

4 Evaluate a Television Program

Evaluate a program made for television or the Internet. It can be a reality show or a regular scripted program. To help students understand what the show is about, use the past tense to describe the types of events that happened in past episodes. What are the strong and weak points of the show? End with a prediction about the show's future.

SPEAKING PRESENTATION TIPS

- **PRACTISE YOUR PRESENTATION** and time yourself. You should speak for about three minutes or for a length determined by your teacher.
- **USE CUE CARDS.** Do not read! Put about fifteen words on your cue cards.
- **BRING VISUAL SUPPORT** such as an object, drawing, poster, photograph, or PowerPoint presentation, or create a short video.
- **CLASSMATES WILL ASK YOU QUESTIONS** about your presentation. You must also ask classmates about their presentations. Review how to form questions before your presentation day.

Revising and Editing

REVISE FOR AN INTRODUCTION
EDIT FOR VERB TENSE AND PREPOSITIONS

A piece of writing should begin with an introduction that captures the reader's attention. (To learn more about introductions, see page 149 in Writing Workshop 3.)

Read the short essay and follow these steps.

1. Underline and correct eight verb tense errors. Also, add a missing preposition.

2. Write a short introduction. Begin with general or historical information, an anecdote, a definition, or a contrasting idea. End your introduction with a thesis statement. The thesis statement expresses the main focus of the essay.

The Importance of Music

Introduction: _____
_____
_____
_____
_____

First, music brings people together. People share songs, talk about the singers, and dress like their idols. For example, in the early 2000s, my brother loved Eminem. He played his *Slim Shady* CD every day. At that time, Eric always has a baseball cap on his head. He weared big pants with a 36-inch waist, but he was very skinny. His pants often fall down when he was walking. Eric's friends dressed the same way. My older sister Kara had a goth phase. She liked to wear black, and she felt like part of a group. There was always a lot of people at her goth parties.

Also, music helps people survive difficult moments. A few years ago, when my friend Melissa broke up with her boyfriend, she listened Justin Bieber. The music maked her feel better. Another friend, Matt, had a difficult time when he was in high school. His father would not accept that Matt was gay. During that period, Lady Gaga's song "Born This Way" helped Matt a lot. Today, he feel self-confident and happy.

Music is important to every generation. It bond people. It also helps people to get through difficult moments. Human beings will always make music.

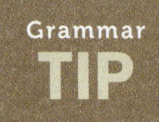

Was or Were

In the past tense, use **was** when the subject is *I*, *he*, *she*, or *it*. Use **were** when the subject is *you*, *we*, or *they*.

      were
There ~~was~~ only one hundred songs on my first iPod.

To learn more about past tense verbs, see Unit 3 in *Avenues 2: English Grammar*.

PART 2
CONSUMPTION AND TECHNOLOGY

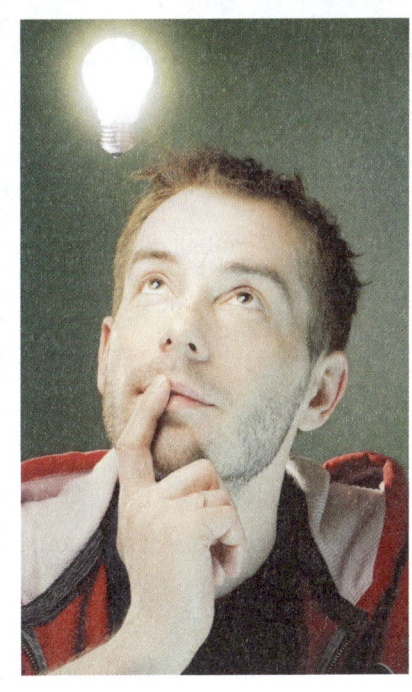

CHAPTER 4

"The more alternatives, the more difficult the choice."
– ABBE D'ALLAINVAL, WRITER

Great Ideas

Every day, we see advertisements that tempt us with a multitude of choices. In this chapter, you will read about some product trends and cult brands.

60	**START UP**	What's the Trend?
61	**READING 4.1**	Novelty Items
63	**WATCHING**	Damn Heels
65	**SPEAKING**	Name That Product
65	**READING 4.2**	The Allure of Apple
68	**LISTENING**	Generic Brands
69	**SPEAKING**	Great Decisions
70	**TAKE ACTION!**	
71	**REVISING AND EDITING**	

START UP: What's the Trend?

PART A
Look at the three clues. Then try to guess the name of the game or trend.

	Clues			Product
EXAMPLE:	exercises	large ball	stretch	Pilates
1	friend me	status update	my wall	
2	cube	colours	match the sides	
3	screen	e-reader	Apple	
4	flat	throw it	resembles a plate	
5	video game	brothers	Luigi	
6	Nintendo	physical	sounds like "yes" in French	
7	jump on lights	dance	arcade game	
8	puzzle	numbers	Japanese	
9	sneakers	wheels	glide	
10	video game	warfare	Call …	
11	kick	sand-filled bags	knees	
12	phone app	game	birds	

Practise clothing vocabulary.

PART B
With a partner, think of at least three other popular trends from the present or past. Consider games, household items, shoes, and clothing styles.

_____
_____
_____
_____

READING STRATEGY

Identifying Main Ideas and Writing a Summary

Identifying Main Ideas

The main idea is the principal focus of a text. It can be expressed in the title, introduction, or conclusion. Look for a **thesis statement**, which is a sentence that expresses the main idea. The thesis is usually at the end of the introductory paragraph.

An essay is supported with facts and examples. Generally, each body paragraph has a **topic sentence**. The topic sentence supports the thesis and expresses the main idea of the paragraph.

Sometimes authors do not write thesis statements or topic sentences. If you cannot find a statement that contains the main idea, then ask yourself *who, what, when, where, why,* and *how* questions. In a sentence or two, you can write your own statement of main idea.

Writing a Summary

When you summarize, you condense a message to its basic elements. You restate what the author said using your own words.

How to Summarize

- Identify the author and the title of the source that you are summarizing. Later, you will include this information in the first sentence of your summary.
- Read the original text carefully. You will need to have a complete picture before you begin to write. Highlight the main and supporting ideas.
- Write your summary. You can keep common words and the names of people and places, but find synonyms for other words.
- Verify that you used your own words and did not copy any phrases or sentences from the text. Also, do not include your opinion.

Important: Avoid Plagiarism

If you copy phrases and sentences from another work, it is considered plagiarism. When you use the exact words of the author, put them in quotation marks and mention the source.

PRACTICE

Write a two- or three-sentence summary of the following paragraph.

> These days, without paying a cent, Facebook users can download a new breed of social game such as Farmville. So how do gaming companies make a profit? It's simple. First, they hook the players. In Farmville, players work on virtual crops, and the crops will die if users don't tend them. After players become obsessed—and millions do—they start paying for items. For example, Mafia Wars users pay for virtual guns, and Farmville players buy scarecrows or virtual plants. Last year, Zynga Inc. earned over $200 million from Farmville.
>
> Adapted from Kohler, Chris. "Farm Wars." *Wired*. Condé Nast Digital, 19 May 2010. Web.

Summary:

_____

_____

_____

_____

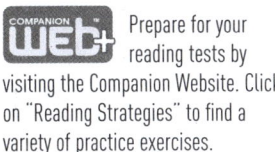 Prepare for your reading tests by visiting the Companion Website. Click on "Reading Strategies" to find a variety of practice exercises.

 Read about various gadgets that are meant to elicit laughter.

Novelty Items

BY A. ROTH

1. I am a novelty item nerd. I got my first rubber chicken when I was a kid. With my limited allowance, I bought myself a pair of chattering teeth and a snake that pops out of a can. When I was a little older, I bought my father a Big Mouth Billy Bass, which he hung in his kitchen until my mom "accidentally" hit it with a hammer. Novelty items—those little seemingly useless joke items that become popular and sell millions of units—have interesting stories behind them.

A whoopee cushion

2 Some of the best gag items are based on gross bodily functions. Realistic looking dog poop and vomit still sell millions of units. In the 1950s, the fake vomit was invented by an employee at a Chicago design company. Glass, of Marvin Glass and Associates, hated the fake vomit. But after he had made an unsuccessful product presentation to a novelty item client, the vomit's creator slapped the fake vomit on the table in the hopes that his creation would cause a stir. Laughs followed, and a new novelty item was born. And who can forget the whoopee cushion, invented in 1930 by employees of a Toronto rubber company—showing that even then, Canadians were always on the cutting edge of comedy[1]. The whoopee cushion had a simple design: two rubber sheets were glued at the edges, with an opening for air to escape. Let's face it: flatulence is always funny. Judd Apatow and the Farrelly Brothers have made millions of dollars on this simple fact. The product continues to be popular and still makes people chuckle.

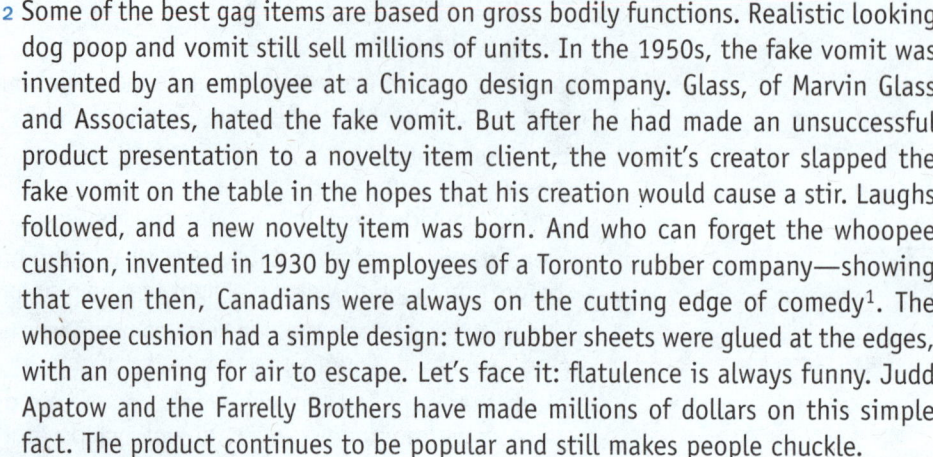

3 Big Mouth Billy Bass, the singing fish that my mother smashed, was invented by Joe and Barbara Pellettieri. In 1998, the Pellettieris, owners of a novelty item company, were discussing product ideas when they passed by a fishing shop in Grapevine, Texas. Barbara looked at the bass on the store sign and thought of a singing fish. Soon after, the company created a thirteen-inch rubber fish mounted on a plaque. Triggered by a motion sensor, the fish's head and tail wave back and forth as the large mouth emits the song "Don't Worry, Be Happy" or "Take Me to the River." In 2000 and 2001, sales of the fish soared and the company earned millions. Although the gag gift had a short lifetime, it became a part of the 2000s pop culture, appearing on the wall of the robot's home in the film *Wall-E*, and showing up in an episode of the popular HBO drama *The Sopranos* and a 2008 episode of *Late Night with Conan O'Brien*.

4 Like many monumental human inventions, some novelty items are created by accident. In the early 1940s, naval engineer Richard James was working with tension springs when one fell to the floor. It kept moving and reforming, appearing to walk across the **deck**. Seeing the potential as a toy, James took his idea to Gimbels department store. He named his product the Slinky, and all of his units sold during a ninety-minute demonstration. Since then, over 400 million units have sold, and you can still find the Slinky on store shelves. Silly Putty was also created accidentally. James Wright, a General Electric scientist, was working on synthetic rubber to use during the war. His mixture of boric acid and silicon oil resulted in a pliable pink substance. Since 1943, Silly Putty has been a popular toy.

deck: floor of the ship

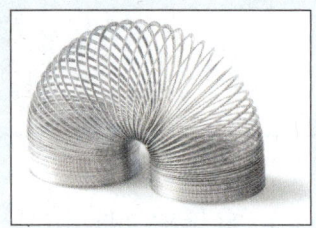
Slinky

5 Why do people create mood rings, doggy sunglasses, and other impractical gadgets? There is serious money to be made in novelty items. Consider this: the Slinky creator became a multi-millionaire from that single product, and since 1950, over 300 million Silly Putty eggs have been sold. In 2005, rubber bracelets with slogans such as Live Strong earned millions, although in that case, Lance Armstrong donated the money to cancer research. Even the creator of the "pet rock," a 1970s novelty item that was exactly what it sounds like, raked in millions of dollars from consumers.

6 In the future, it seems the novelty item is making its way to a hand-held device near you. Recent iPhone apps like the "pull-my-finger" application, which mimics

---
1 Canada is home to many great comedians, including Jim Carrey, Mike Myers, Seth Rogen, and Russell Peters.

the sound of a fart when you touch the finger, show that the spirit of the novelty item is still alive and well (and that flatulence is, indeed, always funny). Now, instead of creating fake vomit out of plastic, some ingenious mind is surely figuring out a way for your phone to mimic the sound of vomiting so you can spook your friends. It's a brave new world.

(750 words)

Sources: Schuessler, Heidi. "Getting Under the Skin of a Fish." *The New York Times*. The New York Times Company, 14 Dec. 2000. Web.
Murray, Steve. "Gag Orders." *National Post*. Canwest Media, 30 March 2011. Print.

VOCABULARY

1 Choose the letters of the best definitions. The paragraph numbers are in parentheses.

Terms		Definitions
1. cause a stir (2)	_____	a. laugh
2. glued (2)	_____	b. increased dramatically
3. chuckle (2)	_____	c. joined with an adhesive substance
4. soared (3)	_____	d. create excitement
5. raked in (5)	_____	e. scare
6. spook (6)	_____	f. collected

2 In paragraph 1, why is *accidentally* in quotation marks?
(Hint: Consider how the mother felt about Big Mouth Billy Bass.)

_____

_____

Answer additional reading and listening questions. You can also access audio and video clips online.

MAIN IDEA

3 Reread paragraph 1. Highlight a sentence that sums up the principal idea of the essay. (That sentence is called a thesis statement.)

4 Underline the topic sentences in paragraphs 2 to 6. The topic sentence sums up the principal idea of the paragraph. Be careful, because the topic sentence is not always the first sentence in the paragraph.

WRITING

Write a summary of the article "Novelty Items." Your summary should be eight to ten sentences long. First, identify the author and the title. Then, using your own words, sum up the main point of the entire essay and the main focus of each body paragraph. Follow the summary-writing guidelines on page 61.

 # Damn Heels

On *Dragons' Den*, aspiring entrepreneurs pitch their business concepts and products to a panel of Canadian business moguls. Watch the episode and answer the questions.

1 What are Damn Heels? Describe the product.

_____

_____

_____

CHAPTER 4 | Great Ideas | **63**

Kevin　Jim　Arlene　Robert　Brett

2 What is the name of the woman who invented the product?
a. Hailey Coleman
b. Hailey Johnson
c. Hailey Smith

3 How many sizes do the ballet slippers come in?
_____

4 About how many units of Damn Heels has Hailey sold?
a. 200　　　　　b. 700　　　　　c. 3000

5 How much does one unit of Damn Heels cost?
_____

6 Which dragon made the first offer?
a. Jim　　　　　b. Robert　　　　　c. Arlene

7 Where are the main competitors to Damn Heels located?
a. France　　　　b. United States　　　　c. the UK (United Kingdom)

8 What did Arlene offer?
a. $25,000 in cash and $25,000 in marketing expertise
b. $50,000 in cash
c. $50,000 in marketing expertise

9 What royalty rate did Arlene want? _____

10 What did the other dragons think about Arlene's deal?
_____

Vocabulary BOOST

Descriptive Adjectives

Write descriptive words under each photo. Choose from the words in the list, and use each word once. Consult a dictionary if you don't understand a term.

Shape and size:　circular　　flat　　hollow　　skinny　　tiny
Touch:　　　　　　cuddly　　hard　　rough　　sticky

1
_____
_____

2
_____
_____

3
_____
_____

Visit the Companion Website to practise more descriptive terms.

SPEAKING

Name That Product

Work with a partner and come up with the names of five pop[ular] games. They can be products from the past or present. As y[ou] think about games you played as a child, household gadget[s, ...] products.

Write down the titles of the products on small pieces of paper. Then join another pair of students. Those students must take turns guessing what your products are. They can only ask "yes/no" questions.

EXAMPLE:
Is it circular?	Yes
Does it have many parts?	No
Does it go on your finger?	Yes
Does it change colour?	Yes

(Answer: "mood ring")

READING 4.2

Juan Rodriguez writes about popular culture and music for various publications in Canada and the US. In the following essay, he discusses the cult of Apple.

The Allure of Apple

BY JUAN RODRIGUEZ

1 Born to shop, and looking for nirvana in an iMac or iPod or iPhone or iPad, I enter an ultra-sleek Apple Store anticipating a quasi-spiritual experience. It is a place of glass and mirrors and wood and stainless steel that acts as a shrine to the cult of Apple Computer. The store is like a **gleaming** interdenominational church offering a Grand Design for Living that Apple co-founder Steve Jobs called the "digital lifestyle." The **buzz** around Apple products is intense, but the **furtive murmur** inside the store is pure postmodern prayer. No doubt, the cult of Apple is a transformative experience. I've been hooked for twenty years without knowing the first thing about the science behind the computer revolution.

2 Part of the "Apple ecosystem," encompassing 360 outlets in twenty-nine countries, the Apple store is très chic. The ceiling appears higher than it is. The sky's the limit! You don't merely browse the goods in this sacred space. It's more like stargazing: hardware as objets d'art. A pale sea-green glass staircase (patented by Jobs) leads up to where accessories are sold. Apple personnel wear T-shirts over a simple cotton jersey to go with their open no-pressure faces. When you walk into the Apple Store, you feel like you will be taken care of in a cool no-pressure way, and that the experience could potentially turn out to be something akin to ... enlightenment!

3 Those cute PC versus Mac ads on **the tube** remind me of my first encounter with the cult of Apple. My journey in life had taken me, on a whim, to Berkeley, California to hook up with a teenage flame whom I hadn't seen in many years. One of the first things that she advised me to do was dump my PC and get a Macintosh Classic, the beginner computer that even an idiot—or an East Coaster—could operate hassle-free. She took me to BMUG (Berkeley Macintosh Users Group) meetings on the University of California campus that she attended religiously. The large auditorium in the round science building—the Mac cult's church of nerds—was populated by geeks speaking in exotic codes and futuristic tongues.

gleaming: luminous

buzz: attention and excitement

furtive murmur: secretive whispering

the tube: slang term for "television"

crass: crude; unrefined

4 From the get-go, she set up the contrasts: The PC, then typified by IBM, was old, stuffy and hierarchical, *sooo* East Coast. Apple was the West, embodying the American frontier spirit—the digital frontier! Then there was the name itself: IBM refers to International Business Machines, the anonymous and crass anything-at-all-costs business. Apple, on the other hand, is a whole earth digital food inviting you to take a creative bite, like so many artists and designers did. Besides, Steve Jobs was way cooler than Bill Gates, head geek of the Evil Empire. It mattered little that Gates was the same age as Jobs (both were born in 1955), talked the same future-shock lingo and, like Steve, wore a modified Beatles hairdo.

portly: heavy; slightly overweight

smug: self-satisfied

5 Gates went ballistic over Apple's great campaign, PC versus Mac, in which the pompous portly PC's attempt to prove the superiority of his product is frustrated every time while the unassuming, polite, boy-next-door Mac looks on, trying not to be smug. Gates told tech reporter Steven Levy, "I don't know why they're acting superior. I don't even get it. I mean, do you get it? What are they trying to say? There's not even the slightest shred of truth to it!"

6 For years, Steve Jobs was Apple's Svengali-like digital shaman, and we were hooked on his aura. One columnist joked that Americans more keenly anticipated Steve's announcement of the brand-new iPad than they did Barack Obama's State of the Union the night before. Magician David Blaine described Jobs as "the ultimate showman who keeps the audience excited the whole way leading up to the reveal." Just as cult leaders are cloaked in secrecy, Apple employees are sworn to it 24/7. Indeed, media columnist David Carr compares Apple's disciplined way of managing the message to "corporate omerta."

7 Of course, Apple's iconic introductions of new products are a kind of "news theatre" that generates hundreds of millions of dollars in free advertising. "Our secret marketing program for the iPhone (prior to the launch) was none. We didn't do anything," Steve explained. In an interview with *Business Week*, he said, "A lot of times, people don't know what they want until you show it to them." Those were the words of a true cult leader.

9/11: Sept 11, 2001, when New York's World Trade Center was destroyed by two airplanes

8 Jobs's ultimate cultural appropriation was music. The iPod spread sounds in the service of mankind—and, at the same time, stabilized Apple Computer and reinvented the music industry. A simple catchphrase—"1000 songs in your pocket"—was all it took. The first iPod was introduced six weeks after 9/11, arriving to rescue America from its collective depression—just like the Beatles did ten weeks after the assassination of John F. Kennedy. As Jobs told *Rolling Stone* in 2003, "Music is really being reinvented in this digital era. It's a wonderful thing. And in our own small way, that's how we're working to make the world a better place."

9 Of course, Apple has also released the iPad, which could be considered a saviour for the book and newspaper industries. Now call me a spiritualist or a sucker, but I'm possessed by a tingling feeling that my iLife is about to change again. Another visit to the Apple Store is certain.

(894 words)

Source: Adapted from Rodriguez, Juan. "The Allure of Apple." *The Gazette (Montreal)*. Postmedia Network, 20 Feb. 2010. Web.

VOCABULARY AND COMPREHENSION

1 Match the words or expressions in bold with the likely meanings. The paragraph numbers are in parentheses.

Expressions	Definitions
1. I've been **hooked** (1) _____	a. spontaneously; impulsively
2. **on a whim** (3) _____	b. got very upset
3. **hook up with a teenage flame** (3) _____	c. get rid of; discard
4. **dump** my PC (3) _____	d. meet an old girlfriend or boyfriend
5. from the **get-go** (4) _____	e. addicted
6. **went ballistic** (5) _____	f. gullible; easily fooled
7. call me **a sucker** (9) _____	g. beginning

2 Find a two-word expression in paragraph 3 that means "with no problems."

_____

3 Rodriguez compares and contrasts PCs and Macs. What are the major differences?

PC	Mac
_____	_____
_____	_____
_____	_____

4 How is Apple like a cult? List at least three ways.

_____
_____
_____

5 In paragraph 6, why does the writer mention Obama's State of the Union address?

_____
_____
_____
_____

6 What is the writer's opinion of Apple? Does he like the brand? Support your answer with evidence from the text.

_____
_____
_____
_____
_____

DISCUSSION AND WRITING

1 Are you a Mac, a PC, or neutral? Explain why.

2 How do Apple ads manipulate us?

3 What other products have cult followings? List some.

LISTENING PRACTICE

Identify Numbers

Before you listen, review how a large number is broken down.

Look at the number: **7,981,560,214**

The number breaks down as follows:

7	seven billion
981	nine hundred and eighty-one million
560	five hundred and sixty thousand
214	two hundred and fourteen

Practise your spelling by doing dictations.

You will hear nine sentences. Each sentence contains a number. Write down the numbers in the spaces provided. Use numerals, not words.

1. _____   4. _____   7. _____
2. _____   5. _____   8. _____
3. _____   6. _____   9. _____

LISTENING

Generic Brands

If a product remains the number one brand for decades, it risks losing control of its trademark. Many pioneering brands suffered that fate. Just ask the makers of the board game "Monopoly," who lost the right to their own trademark recently. Listen to this segment from *The Age of Persuasion*. Pay particular attention to the numbers that you hear.

COMPREHENSION

1. In what year was kitty litter invented? _____
2. What did Kay Draper originally put in her cat's litter box?
   a. sand   b. ashes   c. both of the answers
3. How much did a bag of kitty litter originally sell for? _____
4. Fifty years after he first started his company, Ed Lowe sold it. How much money did he receive? _____
5. Why did Earl Dixon decide to create the first bandaid?
   a. His wife often cut and burned her fingers.
   b. He cut his finger on a machine at his workplace.
   c. He was an inventor and made many other products.
6. In what year was heroin discovered? _____
7. Who discovered heroin? _____
8. In 1899, Bayer exported heroin to how many countries? _____
9. When was the Harrison Narcotics Tax Act passed? _____
10. When the heroin trademark expired, what new product did Bayer launch? _____

SPEAKING

Great Decisions

Answer the following questions yourself. Then interview a partner. W[rite your]
partner's answers in the spaces provided.

Partner's name: _____

1. What should people consider when they are choosing a career path? List some ideas.

   _____
   _____
   _____
   _____

2. Why did you choose this college? Think of two or three reasons.

   My answer: _____
   _____

   My partner's answer: _____
   _____

3. What are some really good decisions that you have made in your life? List at least three ideas.

   My answer: _____
   _____
   _____

   My partner's answer: _____
   _____
   _____

4. Choose one of your decisions from question 3. What factors did you consider when you made your decision?

   My answer: _____
   _____
   _____
   _____

   My partner's answer: _____
   _____
   _____
   _____
   _____

WRITING

What are some things people should consider when they make an important choice? Write about two things people should consider. Use information about yourself and your partner in your supporting ideas.

CHAPTER 4 | Great Ideas | 69

Grammar TIP

Possessive Forms

When you write possessive forms, ensure that your apostrophe is in the correct position.

Singular: the student**'s** choice   Plural: the student**s'** choices
Irregular plural: the children**'s** decisions

To learn more about possessive forms, see Unit 1 in *Avenues 2: English Grammar*.

Take Action!

WRITING TOPICS

Write about one of the following topics. For information about paragraph and essay structure, see the Writing Workshops on pages 137 to 148. Before handing in your work, refer to the Writing Checklist on the inside back cover.

1 Popular Trends

In an essay, explain why certain novelty items and brands become immensely popular. Why would millions of people suddenly decide to buy a whoopee cushion or change from a PC to a Mac? Provide two or three reasons. For supporting examples, refer to the readings in this chapter.

2 Beliefs

In "The Allure of Apple," Juan Rodriguez compares Apple to a cult. These days, many people no longer follow a particular religion. In an essay, explain how consumerism and/or celebrity worship have replaced religion in our culture. Provide specific examples to back up your points.

3 Consumer Magazine

Work with a team of students. First, visit the companion website and read the text "Advertising Is Everywhere." Then write an article about one of the following topics.

- Describe how advertising is everywhere in your environment. Find examples of advertising in your home, college, and neighbourhood.
- Make a critical evaluation of advertisements for fast food, cars, and alcohol. What lifestyle do the advertisements propose? What dangers do the ads neglect to mention?
- Argue that advertising influences us all. Give examples of ways that you and your friends have been influenced by advertising.
- Describe some overrated brands that get too much attention.

SPEAKING TOPICS

Prepare a presentation about one of the following topics.

1 Product Review

Consider two items that you recently bought. You can discuss small items such as a pair of shoes or an iPod, or large items such as a car. Do reviews of both products. Explain their main advantages or disadvantages. End with a suggestion or a prediction.

2 Popular Trends

A trend is something that is very popular for a short period of time. Present trends from the past, present, and future. First, describe a trend from your childhood. You can describe clothing, shoes, or a hair fashion, or discuss a product such as a game or technological item. Then describe a present trend. Finally, end your presentation by predicting what a future trend will be.

Learn more about spoof ads by visiting the Companion Website.

■ **VOCABULARY REVIEW**

Review key terms from this chapter. Identify any words that you do not understand and learn their meanings.

☐ brand
☐ cause a stir
☐ dump
☐ heels
☐ hooked
☐ gag
☐ glued
☐ gross
☐ on a whim
☐ raked in
☐ trend
☐ wheat

To practise vocabulary from this chapter, visit the Companion Website.

3 *Dragons' Den*

(Optional: Work with a partner or a team of students.)

Think of a new fashion or product and propose it to *Dragons' Den*. As a suggestion, you can combine two pieces of clothing into one, or think of a novelty item that might make people laugh. Be prepared to talk about the following:

a. Describe the best features of your item.
b. Explain who you are marketing your product to.
c. Determine a price for your product.
d. Determine a value for your company. Then decide how much money you need to ask for.
e. Explain how you will promote your item. (Use your imagination.)

You must answer questions about your product. You will also ask other team members about their products. Your team will have a chance to be both the inventors and the dragons.

SPEAKING PRESENTATION TIPS

- PRACTISE YOUR PRESENTATION and time yourself. You should speak for about three minutes or for a length determined by your teacher.
- USE CUE CARDS. Do not read! Put about fifteen words on your cue cards.
- BRING VISUAL SUPPORT such as an object, drawing, poster, photograph, or PowerPoint presentation, or create a short video.
- CLASSMATES WILL ASK YOU QUESTIONS about your presentation. You must also ask classmates about their presentations. Review how to form questions before your presentation day.

Revising and Editing

REVISE FOR SENTENCE VARIETY

A piece of writing should have some sentence variety. In the next essay, combine some of the sentences to form new sentences. Use the following words. You might have to make some changes in punctuation and capitalization. (To learn more about essay structure and combining ideas, see Writing Workshops 2 and 3 at the end of this book.)

so   although   but   because   even though   whereas

EXAMPLE: He wanted to be successful. ~~He~~ , so he started an online company.

Some products are status symbols. In my high school, some rich girls always wore designer clothing. They wanted to be part of the "cool" group. For example, Maria C. bought Prada shoes. The shoes were really

CHAPTER 4 | Great Ideas

expensive. Sometimes, a clique of people all wear the same brand. In high school, one group of boys always wore hoodies from a skater company. The other boys did not wear a specific brand. Also, in high school, many electronic items were status symbols. The latest PlayStation and iPhone cost a lot. My friend Phil always bought those products. People think that they are not brand followers. Most people are influenced by advertising and peer pressure.

EDIT FOR PRONOUNS AND QUESTION FORMS

Underline and correct nine errors. There are six pronoun errors and three question form errors.

Why we buy certain products? How much we are influenced by advertising? These days, marketers want us to feel an emotional connection to a product. Using theirs market research, companies manipulate ourselves in very clever ways. For example, marketing campaigns focus on ours insecurities. What impact an advertisement has on our behaviour? A woman may see an advertisement for cellulite cream, and suddenly she feels worried about his cottage cheese legs. After a man watches a commercial about hair replacement, it affects the way he sees hisself. Other products that make us feel badly about ourself are deodorants, acne creams, and anti-aging products.

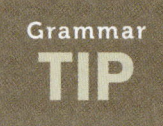

Possessive Adjectives and Question Forms

Possessive Adjectives

Use *his* to show that a male possesses something. Use *her* to show that a female possesses something.

Jonathan loves **his** wife. Isabel buys expensive shoes for **her** son.

Question Forms

Always ensure that your questions have the proper word order.

Question word + auxiliary + subject + verb
　　When　　　did　　　you　　buy that brand?

To learn more about pronouns, see Unit 6 in *Avenues 2: English Grammar*. See Units 2 to 6 for information about question forms.

"For a list of all the ways technology has failed to improve life, please press 3."
– ALICE KAHN, WRITER

CHAPTER 5

The Digital Age

Our world is in the midst of a dramatic shift. This chapter examines our lives in the technological age.

74	**START UP** Tech Life
75	**READING 5.1** My Personal History of E-Addiction
78	**SPEAKING** Addictive Behaviour
79	**WATCHING** Interview with Mark Zuckerberg
80	**READING 5.2** YouTube Hits
83	**SPEAKING** Have You Ever …?
85	**LISTENING** The Peep Diaries
86	**READING 5.3** Gone with the Windows
90	**TAKE ACTION!**
91	**REVISING AND EDITING**

START UP — Tech Life

In the first column, list some things that people did before the technology existed.

Then describe the benefits and disadvantages of the new technologies. Come up with two or three ideas for each item.

Before the Computer Age	Activity	Technology Benefits	Technology Disadvantages
• went to grocery stores • shopped in malls • phoned in orders	**Online shopping** (e.g., eBay)		
	Online social networking (e.g., Facebook)		
	Using a cellphone or smartphone		
	e-Reading (such as with an iPad or Kindle)		

WRITING

Explain how our habits and activities have changed in the computer age.

Present Perfect

The present perfect tense is used to
- describe an action that began in the past and continues today;
  Since the 1980s, computers **have become** common in people's homes.
- describe actions that occurred at unspecified past times.
  I **have seen** the latest iPad, but I do not own one.

To learn more about the present perfect tense, see Unit 5 in *Avenues 2: English Grammar*.

74 | PART 2 | Consumption and Technology

READING STRATEGY

Making Inferences

When you *infer*, you make an educated guess based on the evidence and on your prior knowledge. You make inferences every day. For example, when you see someone wearing designer clothes and driving a BMW, you infer that he or she is wealthy. When your friend doesn't answer your calls after an argument, you can infer that he or she is still angry with you.

You can also make inferences when you read. Sometimes, writers do not state ideas directly. As the reader, you look for clues in the text, and you use your prior knowledge to make your deduction, or educated guess.

PRACTICE

Read the following passage and answer the questions that follow.

> The conditions here are very difficult. We live on tea and hard biscuits, and we receive rations of meat only once a week. The mud covers our boots and clothing, and in some places, the mud and water are up to our waists. We spend our days digging and filling sandbags. We try to drain the dugouts, but our efforts are hopeless as it rains almost constantly. We can hear artillery fire in the distance, but we have not yet encountered the Germans. The waiting causes us much anxiety. We must remain in these trenches for several more weeks.

1. What is the passage about? _____

2. What are some clues that helped you make your guess? _____

Prepare for your reading tests by visiting the Companion Website. Click on "Reading Strategies" to find a variety of practice exercises.

READING 5.1 In the following essay, Steve Almond describes the development of the Internet and his growing addiction to technology.

My Personal History of E-Addiction

BY STEVE ALMOND

1. It took me six days to write this piece, during which—according to the History Tab on my Web browser—I visited 371 websites and checked my e-mail 213 times. I knew the numbers weren't going to be pretty, but I had no idea they'd be quite so ugly. Let me add that I have two small children whose emotional well-being depends on my being an attentive parent. Which reminds me: I need to check my e-mail.

2. Please don't worry. This isn't one of those articles about "How to Kick the Internet." I'm just going to try to relate how I got here.

The Pre-Internet Era (before 1995)

3. Kenny worked as an ad executive at the weekly newspaper where I was a reporter. One day, he started talking about the Internet. "What does it do?" we said.

flushed: red skin showing excitement or emotion

4 His face got all **flushed**. "It's like if someone was coming to, like, Miami, for a vacation and they want to know where to eat or whatever. They plug in an address on their computer and all these pictures and reviews pop up!"

5 We all thought Kenny was crazy. Why would someone go to all that trouble? That's why we had newspapers and guidebooks and telephones! We were simpler creatures then. Computers existed primarily for the compilation and transfer of data, not for entertainment. They were a desk, not a window.

The Library Era (1995–1997)

6 During my grad school years, I spent my days writing wretched short stories that I mailed out to literary magazines. The highlight of my day was walking outside to get "the mail" and its retinue of rejection letters.

7 I don't remember exactly when e-mail entered the picture, but I remember that it required a trip to the library because I had no personal computer. Most of my e-mails were brief notes to my girlfriend, a Polish exchange student who had returned home. I later printed out every note I'd ever received from her so I could have a permanent record.

The Dial-Up Era (1998–2002)

8 During the Internet boom, I moved to a new city. I was slow to make friends. When I look back on this time, I can see that I was an Internet addict waiting to happen: socially isolated, needy, narcissistic, and increasingly computer-dependent. I was part of a growing demographic: those on a slow retreat from the inconveniences of actual life.

9 The only reason I didn't become a full-blown junkie is because I was using a dial-up modem. [One could wait five minutes just for an e-mail to download.] Still, I could feel a shift. Where I used to devote an hour to composing a letter, I was now firing off a dozen electronic notes. I felt a rush every time I opened my inbox. Was someone going to send me a note?

10 It soon devolved into a compulsion. I constantly checked for "good" messages [messages that weren't spam—in those pre-spam-filter days, the inbox could fill up with junk mail]. This e-mail compulsion fortified my isolation. The sound of my old modem, with its symphony of blips, was the song of modern loneliness.

The Wireless Era (2003–2007)

11 Tired of viruses and delays and fruitless conversations with tech support staffers, I bought an Apple. Things went downhill quickly. I started cruising the Net for updates of my favourite sports teams. Then I hunted for news. Then I joined an online dating site. Then another.

lurid: sensational; shocking

12 In previous years, when I felt the sting of solitude, I reached for the phone or for a book. But now I had this vast universe of distraction. Something **lurid** was always happening online. And online, I was a kind of celebrity of my own construction. There were millions of us living in this confused nexus between avatar and identity. We were all **wittier** and better-looking on the Internet.

wittier: more clever or amusing

13 As an author, I could justify my addiction by telling myself I was establishing "an online presence." My computer served as an office, TV, singles bar, and ego masseuse.

ubiquity: omnipresence; being present everywhere

The Era of Ubiquity (2008–present)

14 I comforted myself with the lies of all addicts. *I'm not on Facebook. I only have two e-mail boxes.* But I knew there was something unnatural happening to me. My life was becoming increasingly fragmented. I was spending more time in front of my computer than with the human beings in my life.

15 The outlook of Internet pioneers was utopian and touchingly naive. They saw the "World Wide Web" as a means of building community, democratizing access to data, and speeding its transfer. What they failed to anticipate was the power of capitalism to monetize the medium. The essential currency online is attention—the more eyeballs they get, the more dough companies make. The Internet's job is not to educate or connect us. It is to keep us on a treadmill of ego stimulation.

16 I thought having children would supply a sense of purpose and connection that would render the Internet meaningless. And it did—for the first few months of my children's lives. But I had underestimated how monotonous it is to be a parent. Gradually, I found myself falling back into the old habits.

17 Part of the reason I'm writing this piece now is because I can see that my kids are being affected. My one-year-old, in particular, gets frantic when he sees me or my wife working on the computer. All the kid is asking for is what he deserves: our undivided attention. That connection may be the most precious of our dwindling resources, in the end.

(922 words)

Source: Adapted from Almond, Steve. "A Personal History of E-Mail Addiction." *Salon.com*. Salon Media Group, 14 May 2010. Web.

VOCABULARY

1. In paragraph 2, what does *kick* mean?
   a. to free oneself from a habit
   b. to hit a ball with the foot
   c. a sudden violent movement

2. In paragraph 4, what is the meaning of *plug*?
   a. an electrical outlet
   b. to insert or write
   c. to advertise or promote something

3. Find a word in paragraph 9 that means *addict*. _____

4. In paragraph 15, what does *dough* mean?
   a. flour and water used to make bread
   b. friends
   c. money

5. In paragraph 17, what is the meaning of *dwindling*?
   a. getting larger
   b. expensive
   c. diminishing; declining

Answer additional reading and listening questions. You can also access audio and video clips online.

CRITICAL THINKING: MAKING INFERENCES

6. What is the writer suggesting about life in the Pre-Internet Era?
   a. People were excited about the new computers.
   b. People did not understand the possibilities of computers.
   c. Computers were too expensive for the average person.

7. In paragraph 5, the writer calls computers "a desk, not a window." What does he mean? You will have to read between the lines and make an inference.
   a. Computers sat on people's desks, and they were very large and difficult to carry. They were almost as large as a desk.
   b. Computers did not have the Windows platform.
   c. People thought that computers would provide information like a book that sits on a desk; they didn't realize how computers would connect and inform people around the world.

8. During the Library Era, Almond …
   a. mostly e-mailed his girlfriend.
   b. stopped using the Internet.
   c. had a computer in his house.
   d. All of the answers

9. What can you infer, or guess, about the Dial-Up Era?
   a. The Internet was very slow.
   b. E-mail became very popular.
   c. The writer was not completely addicted to computers yet.
   d. All of the answers

10. During which era did the writer first use e-mail?
    _____

11. In paragraph 15, what point is the writer making about the Internet?
    a. It is a beneficial utopia because it connects people and educates them.
    b. It has become a huge money-generator, and companies basically just want people to keep using their websites.
    c. It does not educate us or connect us.

12. What is the writer's final point? What does he realize?
    _____
    _____

SPEAKING

Addictive Behaviour

Work with a team of four to six students. Write the students' names in the spaces. Include their first and last names.

Partners' names:

_____ _____

_____ _____

_____ _____

Now share information with your group. Be honest. Write the students' initials in the appropriate columns.

How often do you do the following activities?	Rarely or never	Sometimes	Probably too often
Shop for clothing or shoes			
Send text messages			
Drink coffee			
Play video games or online games			
Work out in a gym			
Visit a social networking site			
Watch videos on YouTube			
Drink energy drinks			
Download music and/or movies			

List some of your group's other common habits or addictions:

_____
_____
_____

DISCUSSION

1. What constitutes an addiction? For example, how many hours a day of playing a video game is too many hours?
2. Can addictions be healthy? Think of examples.
3. What are some ways to stop an addiction? Brainstorm some ideas.

WATCHING

Interview with Mark Zuckerberg

Mark Zuckerberg, the founder and CEO of the mega-social media site Facebook, spoke to Lesley Stahl about his life and his business. Watch the interview and answer the questions.

COMPREHENSION

1. Mark Zuckerberg watched the movie *The Social Network*. What did the movie "get right," according to Zuckerberg?

_____

2. How was the movie hot accurate?

_____
_____
_____

3. How did the Winklevoss twins learn about Facebook?
    a. Mark Zuckerberg e-mailed them.
    b. They found the site online.
    c. They read about it in the Harvard newspaper.

CHAPTER 5 | The Digital Age | 79

4. The Winklevoss twins settled out of court. About how much did they win?
   a. $6 million   b. $65 million   c. $165 million

5. Why are the twins still angry with Zuckerberg?
   _____
   _____

6. Do the Winklevoss twins have Facebook pages?   ☐ Yes   ☐ No

7. How does Zuckerberg defend himself? Give two of his arguments.
   _____
   _____
   _____

8. Kara Swisher is the editor of a website about high tech. What is her opinion about the Winklevoss twins controversy?
   _____
   _____

9. In 2006, how much did Yahoo offer for Facebook? _____

10. Why does Zuckerberg not want to sell Facebook? He does not answer the question directly, but make a guess based on his reactions.
    _____
    _____
    _____

READING 5.2 Is YouTube a fast-track to success? Read and find out.

YouTube Hits

Susan Boyle

plain: unattractive

1. How popular is YouTube? In the next minute, over twenty-five hours of video will be uploaded to the popular website. Or to put it another way, in the time it takes you to read this sentence, there will be enough new material on YouTube to waste your whole day. For reasons that are not entirely clear, a few videos will rise above the pack and become viral, reaching millions of viewers around the world. Is YouTube a viable way to get famous? Although some people succeed in obtaining a mass audience, the chances of having a viral video are not very good.

2. Of course, since 2005, YouTube has had a profound impact on some people's lives. Unknown performers have been able to broadcast their abilities directly to the public. Justin Bieber has YouTube to thank for his meteoric rise to fame. In 2007, the twelve-year-old sang for his family, and his mother posted the videos on YouTube. Soon after, Usher and Justin Timberlake competed to sign the kid to their record labels. In another case, in 2011, ten-year-old Maria Aragon caught Lady Gaga's attention when the girl sang "Born This Way" on YouTube. Gaga sent a tweet to her followers, and the video quickly collected nine million views. Arguably the most unlikely YouTube star was Susan Boyle, a **plain**, middle-aged singer and contestant on *Britain's Got Talent*. The producers of the TV program posted the Scottish woman's powerful rendition of "I Have a Dream"

on YouTube. According to Hilary Lewis of *Business Insider*, the video scored 100 million views in a little over a week. Later, Boyle's debut album outsold Rihanna. Such an astounding success story couldn't have happened ten years earlier. Thus, YouTube does make dreams come true—for some people.

3 A viral video seems like a sure way to make money, right? Well, no. In fact, having a video with millions of views doesn't guarantee career success. In "The Flimsiness of YouTube Celebrity," Owen Thomas presents the example of YouTube's first viral video. In 2006, Judson Laipply choreographed a dance routine in his *Evolution of Dance* video. Close to 110 million people saw his clip. However, when Laipply tried to cash in with a career in the entertainment industry, he found 110 million views isn't **all it's cracked up to be**. Today, he sells T-shirts on his website and is working on a public speaking career.

all it's cracked up to be: as great as people say it is

4 Unless you are a superstar, it is difficult—even impossible—to consciously create a viral video. Take the "Double Rainbow" phenomenon. On January 1, 2010, Paul Vasquez filmed a double rainbow. In the video, he gets increasingly excited about the natural phenomenon, moaning "Oh my God! It's so intense!" For six months, the video had just a few hits. Then, in July 2010, it went viral, and quickly gathered more than 30 million views. To this day, Vasquez has no idea why his video suddenly became popular.

odds: chances

5 According to Chris Wilson of *Slate* magazine, the **odds** of purposely creating a viral video are low. In 2009, using Web crawling software, Wilson followed the performance of more than 10,000 uploaded videos to see what would happen. His results show that getting struck by lightning or winning the lottery are more likely to occur than having a video go viral. Wilson writes, "When the odds of even 1000 people viewing your video in a month's time are only 3 percent, it's tough to argue that hitting it big on YouTube is anything more than dumb luck."

aspiring: ambitious and hopeful

6 Still, YouTube provides **aspiring** actors and musicians with a dream. Anyone can bypass record companies and agents and go directly to the fans. If you want to try the YouTube express to fame, there are a few things to consider. First, if you use material that is from another source, including music or film clips, you need to get permission from the copyright holder before you upload the video. Then, ensure that your titles and keywords are accurate and relate to the video's content. The "thumbnail description" (the short description that represents the video) will have a big impact on whether or not people find your video. If it is not accurate, people will be annoyed, and if it neglects to mention your video's best features, people will miss it.

Rebecca Black

7 Some people choose another shortcut to YouTube fame. For a few thousand bucks, you can pay a vanity record label to give you a song and to produce a video. Occasionally the investment pays off. In 2011, the mother of thirteen-year-old Rebecca Black paid Ark Music Factory for two songs and a music video. Rebecca recorded a video for the song "Friday," and the company's producers used auto tune software to disguise any off-key singing. The family posted the video on YouTube and hoped for the best. On March 11, 2011, Black's video inexplicably went from 3000 views to 18 million views. Called "the worst song ever," the "Friday" video has garnered the aspiring singer her own Wikipedia page and a recording contract.

8 People are turning away en masse from scripted television and staged reality shows, and YouTube often provides authentic content from normal people (well, not always normal). So although it is difficult, if you want to express your creativity in a video, go for it. At the end of the day, if a video of a cat playing the piano or people dancing down the aisle at a wedding can become viral, the possibilities truly are endless.

(915 words)

Sources: Lewis, Hilary. "Susan Boyle's Early Audition Tape: The Next YouTube Sensation?" *Business Insider*. Business Insider, Inc., 28 Apr. 2009. Web.
Thomas, Owen. "The Flimsiness of YouTube Celebrity." *Gawker*, 9 Jan. 2009. Web.
Wilson, Chris. "Will My Video Get 1 Million Views on YouTube?" *Slate*. The Slate Group, 2 July 2009. Web.

VOCABULARY AND COMPREHENSION

1. What is a *viral video*? _____

2. In the introduction, highlight the thesis statement. The thesis expresses the main idea of the entire essay.

3. Look in paragraphs 2 to 7. Underline the topic sentence in each paragraph. The topic sentence expresses the main idea of the paragraph. Be careful because the topic sentence is not always the first sentence.

4. What is the difference in meaning between *download* and *upload*?

5. How did Justin Bieber's mother help him achieve fame?

6. Why is Boyle called an *unlikely* YouTube star? _____

7. Why does the writer mention the "Double Rainbow" video? What point does it support?

8. What did Chris Wilson of *Slate* discover when he researched viral videos?
   a. With care and perseverance, anyone can make a viral video.
   b. People who have viral videos probably had dumb luck.
   c. People have a better chance of creating a viral video than of getting hit by lightning.

9. How did Rebecca Black become temporarily famous?

GRAMMAR LINK

10. Paragraph 2 begins with the sentence, "Of course, since 2005, YouTube has had a profound impact on some people's lives." Why is the verb in the present perfect tense (*has had*) instead of the simple past tense (*had*)?

11. Paragraph 7 ends with the sentence, "... the 'Friday' video has garnered the aspiring singer her own Wikipedia page and a recording contract." Why is the present perfect tense used?

   _____

12. What is the past form of *couldn't happen*? Look near the end of paragraph 2 to find your answer.

   _____

DISCUSSION AND WRITING

Discuss the questions and then write about one of the topics.

1. Have you or someone you know ever posted a video on YouTube? If so, what happened?

2. Do you watch YouTube videos? If so, which are the best and worst videos that you have seen? Describe them.

Vocabulary BOOST

Idioms and Expressions

The following expressions appear in this chapter's first two readings. The page and paragraph numbers are indicated in parentheses. Match each expression with its meaning.

Expressions

1. **kick** the Internet (page 75, paragraph 2) _____
2. a **full-blown junkie** (page 76, paragraph 9) _____
3. tired of **fruitless** conversations (page 76, paragraph 11) _____
4. **touchingly naive** (page 77, paragraph 15) _____
5. he gets **frantic** (page 77, paragraph 17) _____
6. **posted** videos on YouTube (page 80, paragraph 2) _____
7. tried to **cash in** (page 81, paragraph 3) _____
8. isn't **all it's cracked up to be** (page 81, paragraph 3) _____
9. **thumbnail description** (page 81, paragraph 6) _____

Meanings

a. complete addict
b. stop using
c. sweetly gullible
d. as great as people say it is
e. useless; unproductive
f. uploaded
g. agitated
h. make money
i. short descriptive summary

SPEAKING

Have You Ever ...?

Compose five questions beginning with the words "Have you ever." Be creative and ask interesting questions about any topic. Then walk around the class until you find someone who answers "yes" to your question. Write the person's name in the space. Include details about the person's experience.

EXAMPLE: Have you ever posted a video on YouTube?
Answer: Alexis has posted six videos on YouTube. His videos show him playing the piano.

Questions:

1. Have you ever _____?

   Answer: _____
   _____

2. Have you ever _____?

   Answer: _____
   _____

3. Have you ever _____?

   Answer: _____
   _____

4. Have you ever _____?

   Answer: _____
   _____

5. Have you ever _____?

   Answer: _____
   _____

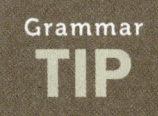

Using *Ever*

Generally, use the present perfect tense with *ever* because you are discussing a life from birth until the present time.

   Have   seen
   ~~Did~~ you ever ~~see~~ the movie *Thor*?

To learn more about the present perfect tense, see Unit 5 in *Avenues 2: English Grammar*.

LISTENING PRACTICE

1. Pronounce *h*, *t*, and *th*

Review how to pronounce *t* and *th*.

PRONOUNCING *T* AND *TH*

When you pronounce *t*, the tip of your tongue touches the roof of your mouth. But when you pronounce *th*, your tongue should touch your top teeth.

   EXAMPLES: tick   thick

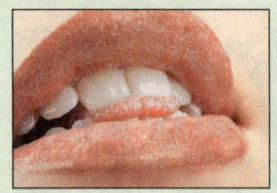

Repeat each set of words after the speaker. Pay attention to the pronunciation of the letters *h* and *th*. Then you will hear a sentence. Indicate the word that you hear.

1	bath	bat	7	math	mat
2	hate	ate	8	fin	thin
3	pat	path	9	truce	truth
4	three	tree	10	tear	there
5	tank	thank	11	sink	think
6	ear	hear	12	taught	thought

2. Pronunciation

Practise your pronunciation by repeating each sentence after the speaker. Then write the missing words in the spaces.

1. The website had _____ thousand hits.
2. My father _____ he lost his keys.
3. Mr. Hall is an _____ hospital worker.
4. We forgot to _____ the teacher.
5. She _____ a math class.
6. There are three tall _____ in the park.
7. He has never _____ a happy moment.
8. Who has reached the _____ level in the game?
9. Harry opened his _____ when he saw a mouse.
10. There are some _____ that we have to talk about.

 Practise your spelling by doing dictations.

LISTENING

The Peep Diaries

Hal Niedzviecki, author of *The Peep Diaries*, created a documentary about online lives. Listen to an interview with Niedzviecki.

COMPREHENSION

1. Niedzviecki compares people who obsessively update Facebook to _____ grooming each other.
   a. children   b. monkeys   c. cavemen

2. The documentary begins with a story about a man named Cork. He broadcasts his life 24/7. What does 24/7 mean?
   _____

3. Why does Cork put his life online? _____
   _____
   _____
   _____

Hal Niedzviecki

4. Why is Hal Niedzviecki skeptical about Cork's online companionship?
   _____
   _____

5. How long did Hal have cameras in his home? _____

6. How many cameras were in Hal's house? _____

7. What was Hal's reaction to being on camera every day?
   _____
   _____

8. Did Hal's wife also agree to be on camera all day? ☐ Yes ☐ No

9. What did Hal dislike about his online experience?
   a. He felt he had no privacy.
   b. He didn't know when he was being sincere or acting for the camera.
   c. He was being contacted by many strange people over the Internet.

DISCUSSION

1. Imagine that cameras followed you around every day. What would you do differently?
2. If you had the choice, would you film your daily life and show it online? Why or why not?

Conditionals

When a sentence suggests an unlikely situation, use the following sentence structure.

If clause (past tense) + Result clause (*would*)
If someone **filmed** my life, maybe I **would act** differently.

To learn more about conditional sentences, see Unit 10 in *Avenues 2: English Grammar*.

Dorothy Nixon is a writer based in Hudson, Quebec. She writes for many newspapers and magazines and is finishing her novel about the life of a woman in the Laurier Era. To read more of her work, you can visit her website *www.tighsolas.com*.

Gone with the Windows

BY DOROTHY NIXON

1. The other day, I had trouble accessing Photoshop through our home network. The program itself was on my other computer, so I had to whip downstairs to see what the problem was. I discovered that my back-up computer was in pieces. My eighteen-year-old had pulled its hard drive apart, no doubt for some mischievous reason, and left the cannibalized carcass to air in the middle of the room.

2 When I asked, "What's up?" he said he needed a component to be able to play a computer game in his room with his friends—and some other people in Japan. Of course, my son has the most advanced computer in the house, by far. He also visits all the usual websites so popular with teens and gets a lot of viruses on his computer. So he is always "wiping his hard drive," as he puts it.

3 I know because he and his dad like to discuss such things. (That's definitely a good thing.) I seldom butt in on these conversations, but the other day I overheard a remark that distressed me. My son was oh-so-casually explaining to my husband how he had inadvertently erased all his photographs from his Grade 11 trip to Europe. The images had evaporated into the ether. All gone. "Not to worry," he said, "Lots of other kids still have theirs."

4 Now, he had taken hundreds of pictures of Baroque fountains and messy hotel rooms and bleary-eyed teens—and shown me the snapshots just once upon his return. I had intended to print out the best ones and mail them to his grandmother. Now she will never see that picture of her grandson Mark with that "gladiator" in front of the Roman Coliseum, the one I call "Marcus Inebrius."

5 Yes, digital technology makes it all just so easy. We can instantly capture our most intimate and spontaneous moments and effortlessly pass these images on to friends and family by e-mail or snail mail or post them on websites for all the wired world to see. And, still, my son's record of his once-in-a-lifetime experience is lost forever.

6 I have a different perspective on things: About two years ago, I found some old documents saved by my husband's ancestors from Richmond, Quebec, in a trunk in my father-in-law's basement. There was a direct-mail ad for Crisco Shortening from 1915, when butter was getting costly. I found a National Drug Company promotional brochure with ads for bizarre remedies such as white liniment for ailments like "brain worry" and "fag" (what we might refer to as chronic-fatigue) and impotency.

7 There were family documents, too. Hundreds of letters were tied up in ribbons. Great Uncle Herb's letters reveal he was always in debt. A newspaper clipping described British militant suffragette Barbara Wylie's arrival in Montreal in 1912. Reporters couldn't believe how attractive a feminist could be!

8 And I discovered booklets containing detailed household accounts. For the 1883 marriage, it cost $5 for a lady's ring and $0.50 for a frying pan. In 1884, after the baby's arrival, a toy cost $0.05 but the doctor's bill was $51! In 1896, a house built in pseudo-Scottish Baronial style went for $2,712. Family expenses for the era averaged between $300 and $500 a year. Wood for heating and dentist and medical bills (outside of childbirth) were the big expenses.

9 We're talking a lot of history here, of interest to family as well as to historians. I posted my findings on the Web and the information has been very well received by the academic community. Some scholars have actually thanked me for making the effort. It was just luck, I tell them, that one day, while waiting for the washing machine to end its spin cycle, my gaze rested on an old Victorian trunk in a basement where I'd been hundreds of times before. I got curious.

10 Will future amateur historians be as lucky as I was? With all the runaway digital documentation going on in homes today, will today's family history be available or accessible to future inquiring minds like mine? I mean, new Web platforms are arising every month!

11 We just recently transferred our baby videos to CD, but it's possible that in a few years the CD format will be as impenetrable as a **cuneiform tablet**. My son's experience with his high-school pictures suggests that a lot of twenty-first century family history could be, well, gone with the Windows. And that will indeed be ironic—and a great big shame.

(763 words)

cuneiform tablet: ancient text inscribed on stone

VOCABULARY AND COMPREHENSION

1 Choose the letters of the best definitions. The paragraph numbers are in parentheses.

Terms
1. whip (1) _____
2. butt in (3) _____
3. messy (4) _____
4. luck (9) _____
5. shame (11) _____

Definitions
a. interrupt
b. cause for regret
c. good fortune
d. rush; move quickly
e. disorderly; untidy

2 In paragraph 1, the writer says that her son "left the cannibalized carcass to air in the middle of the room." What is she referring to?

3 What does it mean to "wipe your hard drive"? See paragraph 2.

4 Where did the writer find the old trunk?

5 What type of information did the old trunk contain?

6 How was the information in the trunk of value?

7 What is the main idea of this essay? What point is the writer making about the digital age?

8 Why is it important to have records of everyday events?

WRITING

On a separate piece of paper, write ten questions that you would like to ask the writer. Use three different verb tenses in your questions.

Tech Game

Look at the word clues to complete the crossword puzzle. Write the technology terms in the spaces corresponding to the numbers. Use a dictionary if needed. Note that 15 across has been done for you.

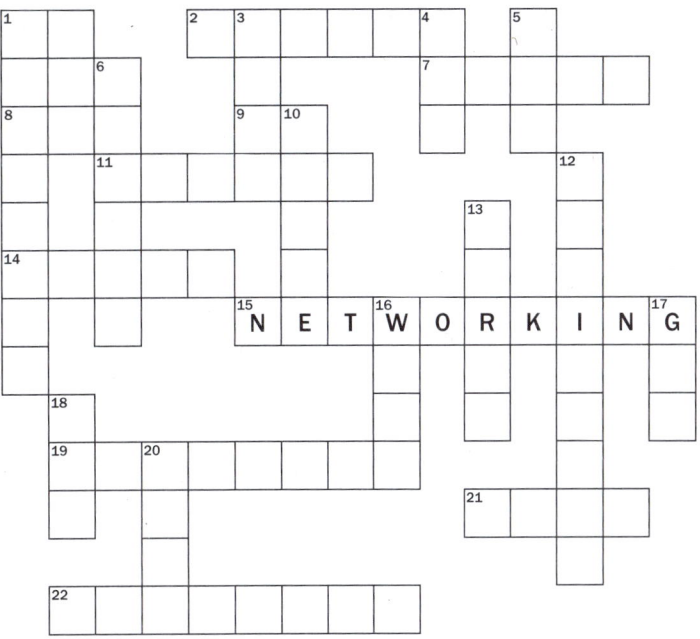

Across
1. The opposite of "down."
2. You read and watch images on this part of the computer.
7. This is a book that is published on the Internet.
8. File Transfer Protocol abbreviation
9. This means "ante meridiem" and refers to the time period from midnight to noon.
11. This small computer can be folded and easily transported.
14. Electronic mail
15. Facebook is a social ___ site.
19. You use this secret word when you log on to a website.
21. This word, formed from *web log*, refers to an online journal.
22. Computers have hardware and ___.

Down
1. On Facebook, this word means "to remove someone as a friend."
3. The Internet is full of ___ rooms. People communicate with strangers in these rooms.
4. This is the short form of *Internet*.
5. In a text message, this means "laughing out loud."
6. This is the opposite of *download*.
10. This device, used with desktop computers, helps you navigate on a webpage. The word also means "a small rodent."
12. Steve Almond developed an ___ to the Internet. He can't stop going online.
13. This destructive computer program can reproduce itself and damage computers.
16. This popular computer software is used to write documents.
17. A ___ helps you navigate through cities.
18. This is the short form of *application*.
20. This word means "to look at various websites." It also means "to ride a board on the waves."

Take Action!

WRITING TOPICS

Write about one of the following topics. For information about paragraph and essay structure, see the Writing Workshops on pages 137 to 148. Before handing in your work, refer to the Writing Checklist on the inside back cover.

1 Social Media

Critique a social media site such as Facebook. What are its benefits? What are its disadvantages? Support your points with examples from your life or the lives of people you know. Also refer to the readings or the video from this chapter. End with a prediction about the future of social media.

2 Oversharing

Oversharing means "to provide too much information about yourself." What are two possible problems with oversharing online? Include specific examples in your body paragraphs. For instance, you can use examples from the media, from your life, and from this chapter's readings.

3 Internet Addiction

Write an essay about the causes and/or effects of an Internet addiction. Provide at least two supporting ideas and include specific examples from your life and from the reading, "My Personal History of E-Addiction."

4 Going Digital

In "Gone with the Windows," Dorothy Nixon identifies a problem with digital photography and the fact that it can be lost easily. What are some other effects of our digital lifestyles? List some examples of technology and the impact it has on our lives. To illustrate your points, use specific examples from your life and from readings in this chapter.

5 Facebook

In the video, "Interview with Mark Zuckerberg," you received a glimpse into Facebook's headquarters. What mistakes or smart decisions has Zuckerberg made? Develop your essay with two or three ideas. In your body paragraph, refer to the video and/or to any relevant readings.

SPEAKING

Prepare a presentation about one of the following topics.

1 Bad Habits and Addictions

An addiction is a behaviour that a person feels compelled to do too often. Describe a bad habit or an addiction that you had in the past, and describe a current bad habit or addiction. For example, you can be addicted to video games, a type of food, Facebook, a type of music, text messaging, caffeine, energy drinks, and so on. End your presentation with a prediction.

2 Technology Fast

Begin by describing the place of technology in your life. What electronic items do you use? How often do you use them?

Then try to spend one day without using your cellphone or computer. Describe what happened. How long did you last without using that technology? End by predicting how you will use technology in the future.

■ VOCABULARY REVIEW

Review key terms from this chapter. Identify any words that you do not understand and learn their meanings.

- ☐ addicted
- ☐ aspiring
- ☐ device
- ☐ dwindling
- ☐ era
- ☐ frantic
- ☐ lurid
- ☐ otherwise
- ☐ the odds
- ☐ unlikely
- ☐ wireless
- ☐ workaholic

 To practise vocabulary from this chapter, visit the Companion Website.

3 Tech Reviews

Work with a small group of students and brainstorm some popular technological inventions (iPad, smart phones, etc.) and some popular websites. Then choose a topic and critically evaluate it. (Each student must choose a different topic.) In your evaluation, discuss the following:

- Who created the site or item?
- What human need does the site or item fulfill?
- How is the site organized? Is it difficult to navigate? How complicated is the item to use?
- What are some positive and negative points about the site or item?
- Make a prediction about the durability of this site or item.

> **SPEAKING PRESENTATION TIPS**
>
> - PRACTISE YOUR PRESENTATION and time yourself. You should speak for about three minutes or for a length determined by your teacher.
> - USE CUE CARDS. Do not read! Put about fifteen key words on your cue cards.
> - BRING VISUAL SUPPORT, such as an object, picture, poster, photograph, or PowerPoint presentation, or create a short video.
> - CLASSMATES WILL ASK YOU QUESTIONS about your presentation. You must also ask your classmates about their presentations. Review how to form questions before your presentation day.

Revising and Editing

REVISE FOR TRANSITIONAL WORDS AND PHRASES
EDIT FOR MIXED ERRORS

Your writing should be coherent. In other words, connections between ideas should be logical. Transitional words and expressions help the reader follow the ideas. (To learn more about coherence, see page 152 in Writing Workshop 3.)

Read the short student essay and follow these steps:

1. Underline and correct eight errors. Look for mistakes with verb tenses, plurals, and pronouns.
2. Add logical transitional words and expressions. Choose from the words provided below. Use each word once.

| first | furthermore | in fact | of course |
| for example | however | meanwhile | therefore |

Raoul does not like to leave his computer. _____, he can easily sit for ten hours in front of that machine. He doesn't see the sun outside or hear the birds. Sometimes, he does not eat or drink. He just

CHAPTER 5 | The Digital Age | 91

types on his keyboard. He thinks he is normal. _____, he is a computer addict. The Internet causes two big problems in our lives.

_____, people share too much information on their social networking sites. _____, there is the story of Ashley Payne. The twenty-four-years-old teacher lost his job because she put a picture of her drinking beer on her Facebook page. Some students saw the image and their parents complained. Since then, Payne been unable to get another teaching job.

_____, after a photo is in cyberspace, it is very difficult to get the photo back. Jasmine Arden used her cellphone to sent a nude photo to her boyfriend. She didn't realized the consequences. After they broke up, her boyfriend put the photo online. _____, Jasmine was furious. _____, people with other websites copied the photo. Her ex-boyfriend agreed to removed the photo, but it was too late. Now Jasmine cannot make the photo disappear. She have learned to be more careful.

_____, people should be vigilant about the information that they share online. They should not post embarrassing photos on the Internet. They should always remember that a picture is worth a thousand words.

Base Form of the Verb

Always use the base form of the verb after *did* and *to*. The base form is the form you find in dictionaries. It has no –s or –ed ending.

             use   call
She didn't ~~used~~ her cellphone. She decided to ~~called~~ with Skype.

To learn more about verb forms, see Units 2 to 6 in *Avenues 2: English Grammar*.

PART 3
URBAN ISSUES

"Space and light and order. Those are the things that humans need just as much as they need bread or a place to sleep."
— LE CORBUSIER, ARCHITECT

CHAPTER 6

Urban and Suburban Life

Do you love modern architecture with its sleek lines, or do you prefer designs from the past? What are some problems with urban sprawl? In this chapter, you will consider architecture as well as urban and suburban life.

94	**START UP** The Ideal House
95	**READING 6.1** Architecture Matters
98	**WATCHING** The End of Suburbia
99	**READING 6.2** The Utopian Town of Celebration
102	**SPEAKING** Living Environment
103	**LISTENING** Littering
104	**SPEAKING** Public Service Announcement
105	**READING 6.3** Chaos in the Streets
107	**TAKE ACTION!**
108	**REVISING AND EDITING**

START UP

The Ideal House

Work with a team of about four students. Take turns talking, without stopping, about the following photographs. Change speakers when your teacher flicks the lights.

When it is your turn to speak, talk about the following topics. You can change your topic at any time during your turn.

1. Which house do you like the most? Why?
2. Which houses do you find ugly? Why?
3. What is the ideal house design? In your opinion, what are the best exterior and interior features?

A. Modern Suburban House

B. City Condominium (condo)

C. Traditional Victorian House

D. Farm House

WRITING

Write a paragraph of about 120 words. Describe what your ideal house would look like. Would it look like any of the houses in the photos? Describe the interior and exterior of your ideal house. Explain what features it would have.

Grammar TIP

Using *Would*

Use *would* to suggest a desire. Use the base form of the verb after *would*.

                    have
My ideal house would ~~has~~ large windows.

To learn more about conditional forms, see Unit 10 in *Avenues 2: English Grammar*.

Exteriors

On the lines provided, write the following vocabulary terms.

| driveway | grass | railing | shutters | steps |
| cement walkway | hedge | roof | siding | yard |

To practise more house-related vocabulary, visit the Companion Website.

How important is design? What are the considerations architects must make when designing a building? Read about architecture and its aesthetic importance.

Architecture Matters

BY LYNNE GAETZ

Gaudí's Casa Mila

1 A few years ago, a pair of Japanese researchers investigated how beauty can influence people. Masaaki Kurosu and Kaori Kashimura asked 252 subjects to rate the usability of objects. In one experiment, they asked people to use two different bank machines. The machines had exactly the same numbers of buttons and the same functions, yet users consistently judged the nicer looking machine to be easier to use. Another researcher, Noam Tractinsky, decided to repeat the experiment. Suspecting that the Japanese have a higher interest in aesthetics than people from other cultures, he replicated the experiment in Israel. To his surprise, the Israelis rated the beautiful machines with higher scores than the Japanese had given them.

2 Design matters.

3 We buy an Apple computer because the design is sleek. We love a new car because the colour and style are striking. And we choose a home with a front porch and shutters because it appeals to our senses. Among everything that surrounds us, architecture can provide the most visible example of aesthetic magnificence.

4 Great architecture affects us emotionally. It lifts our spirits, inspires awe, or simply makes us feel cozy and protected. Designers spend a great deal of time considering proportion, scale, texture, materials, shapes, and light. The best architects create works that inspire and uplift us. For instance, Spanish architect Antoni Gaudi broke from rigid lines and created buildings with walls and balconies that undulate, such as the Casa Mila. "The straight line belongs to men, and the curved one to God," Gaudi once said.

Sydney Opera House

5 In *The Art of Being Human*, Richard Paul Janaro says, "The fundamental issue in determining whether a given architectural work can be labelled 'art' is the interplay of form and function. The function of a building is to accommodate the needs of the inhabitants." So an office space should provide employees with pleasant surroundings that make work less dreary. The design should be sensible, with easily accessible spaces that employees will use during the day. In "The Allure of Apple," Juan Rodriguez praises the design of Apple stores, calling them "sacred spaces" with white walls, high ceilings, and sea-green glass staircases. According to Janaro, "A religious edifice such as a cathedral or temple should be imposing and awe-inspiring, so worshippers can believe that they have left the familiar world and entered a different higher place."

6 Those who design structures often have conflicts with those who use them. And of course, art is subjective, so an architect's vision might be reviled by some and celebrated by others. For example, when Jorn Utzon presented his original designs for the Sydney Opera House, he initially faced formidable opponents, including some high-profile politicians. When the Opera House was completed in 1973, various local journalists and citizens criticized the building, calling it an eyesore. Yet a few years later, it was labelled one of the twentieth century's most distinctive buildings, and UNESCO named it a world heritage site.

Montreal's Olympic Stadium

7 Another building suffered the opposite fate. Although Montreal's Olympic Stadium was initially praised for its bowl-like design and soaring tower, the building's form surpassed the function. It looks striking and original, but Montreal's football team abandoned the stadium after the roof developed ongoing problems and after a concrete block broke off the structure and crashed to the pavement.

8 Of course, architecture also reflects the era in which it was built. Wealthy and powerful kings and queens in past empires were responsible for ordering the construction of magnificent sites such as Versailles, the pyramids, and the Vatican. Today, glass and steel towers reflect our technological age, when people are busy multi-tasking. Some skyscrapers bring to mind the clean lines of our iPads, cellphones, and laptops.

9 Unfortunately, in the frenzy to build cheaply and quickly, many houses, buildings, bridges, and highways are constructed seemingly without aesthetic considerations. James Howard Kunstler, in an article for *The Atlantic*, laments, "We drive up and down the gruesome, tragic suburban boulevards of commerce, and we're overwhelmed at the stupefying ugliness of absolutely everything in sight—the big-box stores,

the office units, the lube joints, the carpet warehouses, the billboards, and the highways clogged with cars, as though the whole thing had been designed to make human beings miserable …. In especially bad buildings, like the average Walmart, windows are dispensed with altogether."

10 Although Kunstler makes a good point about some dreadful designs, architecture remains an art form. It matters. Former British Prime Minister Winston Churchill once observed, "We shape our buildings; thereafter they shape us." The next time you go for a walk in a city centre, take a moment to observe and appreciate the artistry that went into the buildings around you.

(792 words)

Sources: Janaro, Richard Paul and Thelma C. Altshuler. *The Art of Being Human*. Toronto: Pearson, 2008. Print.
Craven, Jackie. "Top Ten Buildings of the Modern Era." *ArchiTechno*, 11 Feb. 2009. Web.
Maleck-Whiteley, Karen. "The Importance of Beauty in Everyday Life." *The Signal.com*, 19 Mar. 2010. Web.

VOCABULARY AND COMPREHENSION

1. Find a word in paragraph 5 that means "boring; dull." _____

2. In paragraph 5, what does *sensible* mean?
   a. emotional   b. beautiful   c. showing good sense

3. Find a word in paragraph 6 that means "something that is ugly; not pleasant to look at." _____

4. In paragraph 6, what does *formidable* mean?
   a. wonderful   b. intimidating   c. desirable

5. In this essay about architecture, why does the writer begin with a study about bank machines?
   _____
   _____

6. List some of the beautiful and inspiring buildings mentioned in the article.
   _____
   _____

7. Name three problematic or ugly buildings listed in the article. Explain the problem with them.
   1. Building: _____
      Problem: _____
   2. Building: _____
      Problem: _____
   3. Building: _____
      Problem: _____

8. According to this text, why is architecture important? Use your own words to sum up the ideas.
   _____
   _____
   _____

WATCHING

The End of Suburbia

How have cities developed since the nineteenth century? Has the growth of suburbs been a good thing? Serious questions are emerging about the sustainability of the suburban way of life. In this excerpt from a documentary, you will learn a short history of suburban development.

COMPREHENSION

1. At the end of the nineteenth century, why did people want to leave industrial cities?

   _____

2. What were the three main stages of suburban growth? Give some key features of each stage.

   1870s to 1900: _____
   _____
   _____

   1920s: _____
   _____
   _____

   1940s: _____
   _____
   _____

3. In the late 1940s, there was a housing boom. What is a *boom*?
   a. a huge increase   b. a dangerous explosion   c. an ending

4. Why does James Howard Kunstler call the typical suburban home *a cartoon of a house*?
   _____
   _____

5. What are some problems with current suburbs?
   _____
   _____

6. Why did GM and Firestone buy up light rail transit lines and streetcar lines?
   _____
   _____

7. How is "New Urbanism" different from traditional suburbia?
   _____
   _____
   _____

8. Why are traditional suburbs not sustainable?
   _____
   _____

READING STRATEGY

Scanning, Highlighting, and Annotating

Scanning means "reading quickly to find specific information." For example, when you want to find a phone number, you scan the phone book. You also scan library books or Internet articles to see if they have information that you need. Your eye searches for keywords or phrases. When you scan, you look quickly for visual clues so that you can determine the selection's key points. Some visual clues include titles or subheadings, photos, charts, graphs, dates, and numbers.

When you read, you may forget some of the author's ideas. To help you find the important points quickly, you can **highlight** key ideas and make **annotations**. These are comments, questions, or reactions that are added to the margins of a page.

Each time you read an essay, follow these steps.

- Highlight sentences that sum up the main idea.
- Underline or highlight supporting ideas. You might even number the arguments or ideas. This will help you understand the essay's development.
- Circle words that you do not understand.
- Write notes beside any ideas that you find particularly interesting.
- Write questions beside ideas that you find confusing.

Prepare for your reading tests by visiting the Companion Website. Click on "Reading Strategies" to find a variety of practice exercises.

READING 6.2

In the mid-1990s, Disney built the "perfect" town. Scan this reading about Celebration, Florida. Highlight main ideas and circle words that you do not recognize.

The Utopian Town of Celebration

BY DOUGLAS FRANTZ AND CATHERINE COLLINS

Celebration, Florida

1. Rarely has a town been conceived and constructed in the glare of publicity and aura of hope that greeted Disney's master-planned, picture-perfect village of Celebration in central Florida. Expectations were so high that, in November 1995, four thousand people entered into a lottery for the chance to win the right to pay 25 percent over the market price to move into one of the first five hundred or so homes.

2. Many of those pioneers expected Celebration to recreate the ideal of Disney World just a few miles away, not for a week-long holiday, but for fifty-two weeks of the year. They thought their children would get straight As at the model school and that there would never be a weed in their lawns. For the solidly middle-class, overwhelmingly white population, this was the adventure of a lifetime, the chance to start over in a town paved with great expectations.

3. Reality seemed to catch up with the utopian village, which Disney gave up control of a few years ago, when residents recently awoke to find that one of their neighbours, a fifty-eight-year-old retired schoolteacher, had been murdered. [Patrick Giovanditto, a well-liked man, lived alone with his Chihuahua.] The yellow crime-scene tape surrounding his condo contrasted with the nearby town square,

which was decorated for Christmas and awash in holiday music from speakers hidden in the foliage. Then, three days later, another resident fatally shot himself after a standoff with sheriff's deputies. [The situation—described as a domestic dispute—involved a man who had lost his job and marriage.] The apparently unrelated deaths showed the world what people in Celebration already knew: life behind the town's white picket fences wasn't perfect after all.

4 We moved to Celebration with our two children in 1997. We were among the first residents, though we arrived with our eyes wide open and a contract to write a book about living in Disney's brave new town. We found out just how strange a place we had chosen when a new neighbour told us that he and his family had considered going to Mexico for vacation, but found they had just as much fun at the Mexico pavilion at Epcot Center at Disney World. Another neighbour—a security guard at Disney—kept a six-foot-high Mickey Mouse in his front window, which our children found a little **creepy**. But there was a spirit of camaraderie that everyone embraced, even we skeptics.

creepy: weird; disturbing

5 The town felt like a movie set. Architects like Michael Graves and Philip Johnson designed its public buildings. Rocking chairs lined the man-made lake in the centre of town; they weren't tied down and they were never stolen. Houses were variations on a limited number of designs, based on the architecture and feel of old coastal villages. They were clustered around parks, with porches hugging the sidewalks to encourage neighbourliness.

6 The community rulebook mandates the colour of the houses and the varieties of plants in the pristine yards. [Some rules are particularly invasive. A maximum of two people can occupy a bedroom. Cars cannot be parked in a driveway for more than twenty-four hours, and must then be stowed away from view in the garage. If residents complain about a pet, the unelected "Celebration Board" can remove the pet without the owner's permission.] Everything spoke softly of small-town America, family values, and safety.

imagineering: blending of *imagination* and *engineering* to describe Disney's invented world

spate: a sudden large amount

7 But long before the schoolteacher's body was discovered, many people in Celebration had already realized that Disney's social **imagineering** couldn't create a bubble of immunity. By the time we moved away in 1999, the pixie dust had begun to fade for some of the diehard believers. There had been a **spate** of divorces, a couple of domestic abuse cases, a handful of stolen bikes, and even an armed robbery.

8 The years have changed the footprint as well, and not for the better. Celebration's initial design of a downtown core to emphasize walking over cars and friendliness over isolation started to disappear even before Disney ceded control. Ever-larger houses have spilled across hundreds of acres of reclaimed swamp, replacing the small-town feel with something closer to traditional suburban sprawl. The town now has about ten thousand residents.

9 There was another kind of blight, too. When we drove down our old street a few months ago to visit friends, two of the sixteen houses stood empty, the paint peeling and the once-pristine lawns burned out in the scorching sun—a story repeated on almost every street in the town. The housing foreclosures that have swept across Florida hit Celebration hard. One real estate Website recently listed 492 foreclosures in town, and housing prices have dropped sharply from the highs of the middle part of the last decade. [One resident, Glenn Williams, said the price

of his home went from $825,000 to $325,000 in a two-year period.] The movie theatre, once a focal point of downtown, shut its doors on Thanksgiving Day.

10 The wave of news coverage that accompanied the violence this week in Celebration says more about society's enduring fascination with the unobtainable vision of utopia than it does about the town itself. Residents there long ago got over the idea that their home was another ride at the Magic Kingdom. They know that not everyone lives happily ever after, even in the town that Disney built.

(888 words)

Source: Frantz, Douglas and Catherine Collins. "It's a Small Town After All." *The New York Times*, 4 Dec. 2010:A23. Print.

DEFINITIONS AND WRITTEN RESPONSE

Do the following on separate pieces of paper.

1. Write English definitions for ten unfamiliar words from the text.
2. Write ten questions and answers about the text. Use complete sentences for your answers.

Lifestyles

Do not confuse these terms.

suburb (noun): an area at the outskirts or edge of a city
suburban (adjective): relating to a suburb
countryside: rural area
town: an urban area that is smaller than a city
urban sprawl: the uncontrolled spread of urban development into the countryside

PRACTICE

Fill in the blanks with the correct words. Choose one of the words listed above.

1. Kendra lives in a _____ in the eastern part of Vancouver. Vancouver is getting very large. Kendra wants to live far from a big city. She hopes to move to a smaller _____ such as Penticton.
2. When people live in _____ areas, they usually need cars to commute to work.
3. We sometimes drive outside the city. Our friends have a cabin in the _____. It is far from civilization.
4. Some environmental activists are worried about _____. It damages wetlands and contributes to the loss of habitat for many animal species.

SPEAKING — Living Environment

Work with a partner or team of students. Debate which is better: living in a city centre, a suburb, or the countryside. Brainstorm advantages and disadvantages for each type of lifestyle.

	Advantages	Disadvantages
City Centre		
Suburb		
Countryside		

WRITING

Write an essay about which lifestyle is better: living in a city, a suburb, or the countryside. Give specific examples of places that you know.

Grammar TIP

Comparatives and Superlatives

Be careful when you use comparative and superlative forms. Generally, when adjectives have one syllable, add –*er* to form the comparative or –*est* to form the superlative.

> Houses were small**er** in the past than they are today.
> Some of the larg**est** houses are in suburbs.

When adjectives have two or more syllables, add *more* to form the comparative or *most* to form the superlative.

> A farmhouse is **more** beautiful than a condominium.
> The subway is the **most** ecological way to travel.

To learn more about adjectives and adverbs, see Unit 9 in *Avenues 2: English Grammar*.

102 | PART 3 | Urban Issues

LISTENING PRACTICE

Identify Contractions

Listen to each sentence. Then underline the words that you hear. Note the following:

- In affirmative sentences, the main verb is stressed.   I will **do** it.
- In negative sentences, the contracted negative verb is stressed.   I **won't** do it.

1	can	can't	7	would	wouldn't
2	can	can't	8	could	couldn't
3	should	shouldn't	9	could	couldn't
4	should	shouldn't	10	can	can't
5	does	doesn't	11	can	can't
6	would	wouldn't	12	are	aren't

 Practise your spelling by doing dictations.

LISTENING

Littering

Why do people litter? What can be done to stop littering? Listen to a discussion about littering with activist Wesley Reed.

VOCABULARY

Listen and fill in the missing verbs and modals in the spaces provided. Write the affirmative or negative form of the words that you hear.

1. Everyone knows they _____ litter, but many do it anyway. So what _____ we do about littering? Listen to the story of a Montreal man. In 2007, Claude Landry _____ walking on a Montreal street with his friend Martin Thibodeau. Suddenly, in front of them, a driver opened his car door and proceeded to empty his car ashtray on the sidewalk.

   Landry _____ believe it. He ran up to the car, picked up the cigarette butts with his bare hands, and _____ them back into the driver's lap. Of course, the driver _____ too happy. He jumped out of his car and chased Landry. The entire event was being filmed by Landry's friend, and the video footage _____ up on YouTube. Claude Landry became the "Cigarette Butt Hero."

COMPREHENSION

2. Wesley Reed grew up in which decade?

   a. 1970s   b. 1980s   c. 1990s

3. When Reed was a child, an anti-pollution television commercial really impressed him. Which character was in the commercial?
   a. A "don't pollute" owl
   b. Bart Simpson
   c. Iron Eyes Cody

4. Where does Reed live now?
   a. In an urban centre
   b. In a suburb
   c. In the countryside

5. According to a poll, which group litters most often?
   a. People aged eighteen to twenty-four
   b. People aged twenty-five to thirty-four
   c. People over sixty-five

6. Who litters the least? _____

7. According to Reed, is a cigarette butt considered litter? ☐ Yes ☐ No
   Explain why. _____
   _____

8. In Singapore, how much do litterers have to pay for a first littering offence? _____

9. In Singapore, what happens to litterers after a second offence?
   _____
   _____

10. In England, what did authorities attach to closed-circuit cameras?
    a. security guards
    b. loudspeakers
    c. face recognition software

11. Do the majority of British citizens support the initiative to catch litterers with security cameras? ☐ Yes ☐ No

12. According to Reed, what can Canada do to prevent littering? List three things.
    _____
    _____
    _____
    _____

SPEAKING

Public Service Announcement

Work alone or with a team of students and prepare a public service announcement to address one of the following issues.

- Convince people to stop littering.
- Convince people to take public transportation instead of driving to work.
- Convince people to use bicycles instead of cars.
- Your choice (related to urban, suburban, or country life)

Your presentation should include a slogan. (A slogan is a short motto used in advertising, politics, and so on. For example, Nike's slogan is "Just do it." During the 2008 US Elections, Barack Obama's slogan was "Yes We Can!")

Use your own ideas. **Do not** borrow ideas from other sources. If possible, videotape your announcement.

READING 6.3 Read about a traffic design theory. Should we get rid of stop signs and red lights and let cars, bikes, and people mingle together?

PRE-READING VOCABULARY
Write the correct word under each photo.

crosswalk   lanes   speed bump   speed limit sign   traffic signal

Chaos in the Streets

BY LINDA BAKER

cringing: recoiling with a feeling of concern

1. It's rush hour, and I am standing at the corner of Zhuhui and Renmin Road, a four-lane intersection in Suzhou, China. Ignoring the red light, a couple of taxis and a dozen bicycles are headed straight for a huge mass of cyclists, cars, pedicabs, and mopeds. **Cringing**, I anticipate a collision. Like a flock of migrating birds, however, the mass changes formation. A space opens up, the taxis and bicycles move in, and hundreds of commuters continue down the street, unperturbed and fatality free.

2. In Suzhou, a city of 2.2 million people, the traffic rules are simple. "There are no rules," as one local told me. Drivers of all modes pay little attention to the few traffic signals and weave wildly from one side of the street to the other. Defying survival instincts, pedestrians have to barge between oncoming cars to cross the roads. But here's the catch: During the ten days I spent in Suzhou last fall, I didn't see a single accident. And despite the obvious advantages that accrue to cars because of their size, no single transportation mode dominates the streets.

3. As the mother of two young children and an alternative-transportation advocate, I've spent the past decade supporting the installation of ever more traffic controls: crosswalks, traffic signals, speed bumps, and speed limit signs in school zones. But I'd only been in Suzhou a few days before I started thinking that maybe there's a method to the city's traffic madness.

Kaifeng, China

4. As it turns out, I'm far from the first person to think along these lines. In fact, the chaos associated with traffic in developing countries is becoming all the rage among a new wave of traffic engineers in Europe. It's called "second-generation" traffic calming, a combination of traffic engineering and urban design. Rejecting the idea of separating people from traffic, it's a concept that privileges disorder over order. In practice, it's about dismantling barriers between cars, pedestrians, and cyclists. "One of the characteristics of a shared environment is that it appears chaotic, and it demands a strong level of having your wits about you," says UK traffic and urban design consultant Ben

Hamilton-Baillie, speaking from his home in Bristol. "Today, we have a better understanding that chaos can be productive."

5 The implications are radical. Hamilton-Baillie argues that the key to improving safety is to remove traffic lights and other controls, such as stop signs and the white and yellow lines dividing streets into lanes. Without any clear right-of-way, he says, motorists are forced to slow down to safer speeds, make eye contact with pedestrians, cyclists and other drivers, and decide among themselves when it is safe to proceed.

6 When it comes to reconfiguring streets as community spaces, ground zero is Holland and Denmark, where some city planners are removing traffic lights, divider lines, and speed limits. Research has shown that fatality rates at busy intersections, where two or three people were being killed every year, dropped to zero when controls and boundaries were taken away.

7 Safety analysts have known for several decades that the maximum vehicle speed at which pedestrians can escape severe injury upon impact is just under thirty kilometres per hour. Research also suggests that an individual's ability to interact and retain eye contact with other human beings diminishes rapidly at speeds greater than thirty kilometres per hour. Combining slower speeds with a reduction in traffic controls, in other words, appears to profit the driver and pedestrian.

8 There's a place for highways and roads dedicated solely to the movement of automobiles, Hamilton-Baillie says. But that place is not in city centres. "[In] the human-controlled world of the city, you pick up your rules not from what you're allowed to do, but from a much more subtle and complex series of codes. If I walk into your living room, I do not need a sign that says, 'Do Not Spit on the Floor,'" he explains. "If there were such a sign, it would probably be counterproductive."

9 The shared-space approach celebrates the complexity and contradictions of city life. The absence of traffic controls means that people are out for themselves; the trick is, they have to look out for everyone else as well. Second-generation traffic design is a curious mix of selfishness and altruism, of order amid chaos. And it just might work.

(730 words)

Source: Baker, Linda. "Why Don't We Do It in the Road?" *Salon.com*. Salon Media Group, 20 May 2004. Web.

VOCABULARY AND COMPREHENSION

1 Find a word in paragraph 2 that means "move in a zigzag pattern."

_____

2 In paragraph 2, what does *barge* mean?
   a. to force oneself in   b. a flat vehicle   c. to interrupt

3 In paragraph 4, find a three-word expression that means "really popular."

_____

4 In paragraph 4, what is the meaning of the expression *having your wits about you*? Read the words in context before you make your guess.
   a. being funny   c. having money in your pockets
   b. having people nearby   d. thinking clearly and being alert

5 What is *"second-generation" traffic calming*? Explain the concept using your own words. See paragraphs 4 to 6 for explanations.

_____
_____
_____

6 Why is "second-generation" traffic design considered safer? How can it be safer if there are no traffic lights, stop signs, or driving lanes?

_____
_____
_____

7 According to designer Ben Hamilton-Baillie, traffic signals and signs should be removed …

a. from all roads.

b. from most city streets, but not from highways.

8 What is the writer's opinion? Does she agree with this new type of traffic design? Explain your answer with proof from the essay.

_____
_____
_____
_____

DISCUSSION AND WRITING

Should your town or city remove traffic lights and stop signs? Would it make streets safer or less safe? Give your opinion.

Take Action!

WRITING TOPICS

Write about one of the following topics. For information about essay structure, see the Writing Workshops on pages 142 to 148. Before handing in your work, refer to the Writing Checklist on the inside back cover.

1 An Educational Institution

Critique your college or university building(s). Suggest two or three improvements. Provide supporting examples and anecdotes to prove your point. Refer to some of the ideas in "Architecture Matters."

2 The Best Living Environment

What is the best place to live: a city, suburb, town, or the countryside? Think of two or three reasons why that place is better than the other alternatives. Give specific examples to back up your opinion. Refer to readings or the video from this chapter.

3 Utopia

Watch *The Truman Show*. The movie came out in 1998, which was several years before reality television and social websites became popular. In an essay, describe two or three ways in which the movie predicted the future. In your body paragraphs, you can refer to readings in this chapter. For example, you can compare Truman's town with Celebration, Florida.

SPEAKING TOPICS

Prepare a presentation about one of the following topics.

1 Compare Architecture
Compare old and new architecture and explain which style is better. Show photos of specific buildings to support your main points.

2 Compare Two Places
Compare two places (for example, two cities or a city and a town). Explain which place you prefer. Give specific supporting examples.

3 Public Transportation
Explain some of the positive and negative points about public transportation in your region. Should there be more trains or subways? Are there enough bike paths? Provide specific supporting examples.

4 Your School
Critique your own educational institution. What are some positive and negative points about your college or university building(s)? Consider the design and layout.

■ VOCABULARY REVIEW
Identify any words that you do not understand and learn their meanings.

☐ billboard
☐ crosswalk
☐ dreary
☐ grass
☐ hedge
☐ housing boom
☐ litter
☐ railing
☐ skyscraper
☐ speed bump
☐ traffic light
☐ urban sprawl

 To practise vocabulary from this chapter, visit the Companion Website.

SPEAKING PRESENTATION TIPS

- **PRACTISE YOUR PRESENTATION** and time yourself. You should speak for about three minutes or a length determined by your teacher.
- **USE CUE CARDS.** Do not read! Put about fifteen words on your cue cards.
- **BRING VISUAL SUPPORT.** You can bring an object, picture, poster, photograph, or PowerPoint presentation, or create a short video.
- **CLASSMATES WILL ASK YOU QUESTIONS** about your presentation. You must also ask your classmates about their presentations. Review how to form questions before your presentation day.

Revising and Editing

EDIT FOR COMPARATIVES AND WORD CHOICE
REVISE FOR A CONCLUSION

A piece of writing should end with a concluding idea. Sum up the essay's main points. Then end with a prediction or a suggestion. To learn more about conclusions, see page 150 in Writing Workshop 3.

Read the following short essay and follow these steps.

1 Underline and correct nine errors with adjectives and adverbs and with *than*, *then*, and *as*.

2 Write a concluding paragraph. It can be three or four sentences long. End with a prediction, suggestion, or quotation.

You can use the following terms to conclude your essay. Put a comma after these expressions.

In conclusion,   To conclude,   To sum up,   Finally,

In the film *The End of Suburbia*, the director argues that suburbs are worst than urban areas because everybody takes a car to work. According to him, people can travel more easier in a city because there is a lot of public transportation. He also says that suburbs have "cartoon houses." But the director is wrong. It is more better to live in a suburb than a city.

First, suburbs are attractive and peaceful. They have more green places then cities. On my street, there are large trees and beautifull flowers. Every morning, I hear birds singing. In the city, there are cements sidewalks and grey buildings. The city is not as beautiful than the suburbs.

Also, cities are polluted. When I spend time in the city, especially during the summer, my skin feels filthy by the end of the day. The air is full of pollution. In *The End of Suburbia*, there is a city scene that shows smoke in the sky above factories. Definitely, cities are more dirtier than suburbs. Cities are the worse place to be in the summer. When I return to my family's suburban house, I can smell the fresh air.

ADD A CONCLUSION

_____
_____
_____
_____
_____
_____
_____

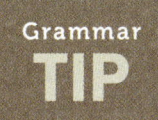

Adjectives

In comparisons, do not add both *more* and *–er* to short adjectives. Also remember that adjectives never take a plural form.

                                                                other
The small blue house is ~~more~~ **nicer** than the ~~others~~ houses.

To learn more about comparative and superlative forms of adjectives, see Unit 9 in *Avenues 2: English Grammar*.

"A riot is the language of the unheard."
— MARTIN LUTHER KING JR., CIVIL RIGHTS ACTIVIST

CHAPTER 7

Social Issues

What are some of the particular problems in urban areas? In this chapter, you will consider urban issues such as crime, riots, and homelessness.

111	**START UP** Crime Scenes
113	**READING 7.1** Flash Mobs, Flash Robs, and Riots
117	**SPEAKING** Flash Mob
118	**LISTENING** Public Shaming
119	**SPEAKING** Crime and Punishment
121	**READING 7.2** The Cop and the Anthem
126	**WATCHING** Ask Me Anything: I'm Homeless
127	**TAKE ACTION!**
128	**REVISING AND EDITING**

START UP

Crime Scenes

Look at the following two descriptions of crimes. Work with a partner or team and try to solve each crime.

CASE 1

On Sunday, May 2, while Mrs. Moon was away, someone opened her safe and stole her diamonds. Police questioned three suspects to ask what they were doing on the day of the theft.

The butler said that it was his day off, so he was playing golf at the time of the theft. He played on an 18-hole golf course. The maid said that she was at the passport office waiting to get her passport renewed. She had to wait for hours in a long lineup. The gardener said that he was in the back garden planting some flower bulbs at the time of the theft. He didn't go near the house.

Detective Smart arrested one of the employees. Who did he arrest? How did he know which employee was lying?

CASE 2

Mr. Reed called the police to report that someone had broken into his office and stolen $10,000 from his desk. Mr. Reed said that when he arrived and unlocked his office door, he saw that the window was broken and his desk drawers were all open: "I had $10,000 in my desk. The thief must have entered and exited through the window."

Detective Ellis checked the scene carefully. On the desk, there was a cup of coffee. The drawers were open and papers were on the floor. The detective put her head out the window. There was broken glass outside, underneath the window, but no footprints were visible because the ground was cement.

Detective Ellis decided to arrest Mr. Reed for insurance fraud. She believed that Mr. Reed was lying. How did she know?

LISTENING PRACTICE

Police Reports

Listen to the two police reports. Draw sketches of the suspects in each space. You don't have to be a good artist; just do your best to show some of the details. Also fill in the blanks with the detailed information about the stolen objects. (For vocabulary related to physical appearance, see Appendix 2.)

Practise face and hair vocabulary.

CASE 1	CASE 2
Suspect	**Suspect**

Case 1:
- Purse brand: _____
- Colour: _____
- Items inside: _____
- Value: _____

Case 2:
- Car type: _____
- Year: _____
- Colour: _____
- Value: _____

Vocabulary BOOST

Crime-Related Vocabulary

Review the crime-related vocabulary.

trial: a case presented before a judge
sentence: a judgment that specifies the type of punishment
witness: a person who saw a crime and gives evidence about it

PRACTICE

Practise using more crime-related vocabulary. Write the letters of the best definitions in the spaces.

Terms
1. jaywalk _____
2. commit arson _____
3. assault _____
4. manslaughter _____
5. shoplift _____
6. kidnap _____
7. bail _____
8. smuggle _____

Definitions
a. money given to a court to ensure that the accused shows up for trial
b. an accidental killing
c. abduct and confine another person
d. illegally cross the street against a traffic light or between marked crosswalks
e. physically attack someone
f. bring contraband items over international borders
g. intentionally set a fire
h. steal from a store

READING 7.1

What makes people riot? And what should happen to rioters? Read and find out.

Flash Mobs, Flash Robs, and Riots

BY DIEGO PELAEZ

1. Have you heard of flash mobs? Groups of people gather in public places to dance with synchronized movements, sing, or have water fights. Some credit Improv Everywhere's "Frozen Grand Central" as the clip that really ignited the flash mob revolution. Uploaded in 2008, the clip shows people milling about New York's Grand Central Terminal. Suddenly, about two hundred people freeze in position, looking like statues. Every year, some cities have flash mob pillow fights. In 2011, in Toronto, a mob gathered in Younge-Dundas Square, and people happily whacked each other with pillows.

2. If an instant party can be planned using social media, why not do something more nefarious? In 2010, American police saw the rise of the "Flash Rob," where large groups of people descended on stores to steal items. In July 2011, a thieving mob descended on an Ottawa convenience store. But shoplifting might be considered **tame** compared to what happened in England a month later. In August 2011, for five days and nights, marauding bands of looters and arsonists showed little compassion as they robbed

Toronto flash mob: public pillow fight

tame: safe and subdued

the stores of their local merchants and set fire to the homes of their neighbours, often with a smile on their faces.

3. Of course, Canada is not immune to rioting. Earlier in 2011, Vancouver hockey fans burned cars and looted stores. But the disappointed hockey fans dispersed once the adrenaline rush brought on by a difficult loss subsided. What happened in England was different. The riots went on for days, moving from one town to the next, as mobile groups organized at the click of a keypad.

4. England's first riot began in Tottenham, an area in North London, where a peaceful protest about a police shooting turned violent. Thus, Tottenham's mayhem may have been about class and race. But as the riots spread, participants in different towns took advantage of the chaos to go on destructive shopping sprees. Paul Lewis, a reporter from London's *The Guardian* newspaper, wrote that disparate groups consulted their BlackBerries to decide where to go next. One fellow was overheard saying, "Let's go rob Hampstead," when his friend responded, "Kilburn, it's happening in Kilburn.'"

England riot

5. Videos of the riot quickly went viral. In one particularly upsetting scene widely viewed on YouTube, a Malaysian exchange student was beaten by a gang of kids. He lay on a sidewalk bleeding, his jaw broken, when a much larger man seemed to help him, gently lifting the boy to his feet. A moment later, the "good Samaritan," along with several other onlookers, reached into the boy's backpack to rob him. Cameras also caught crowds laughing as an apartment building burned. Storekeepers, many who barely make ends meet, saw their windows shattered and their inventory depleted. One shop owner, sobbing, tried to run back into his burning store to save some stock. An uninsured butcher in Tottenham lost about $50,000 worth of meat and worried that this event had destroyed his life's work.

6. So England's riots have taken a toll. Some people have lost their homes, their businesses, and even their lives. Sixty-eight-year-old Richard Bowes was beaten to death merely because he tried to stop rioters from burning down a building, and three people were run over as they tried to defend their neighborhood.

7. At first glance, the rioters were dismissed as young hoodlums, youths from the underclass who need to express their anger in some tangible way. In an article for the *Daily Mail*, Max Hastings wrote, "The people who wrecked swathes of property, burned vehicles and terrorized communities have no moral compass to make them susceptible to guilt or shame." Newspaper headlines called the rioters "amoral uneducated **thugs**."

thugs: cruel and violent criminals

8. Yet a more complete picture of rioters shows that they were of various ages and social classes. Although many of the participants were young and unemployed, rioters also included children, students, and workers who were decidedly middle-class, and who certainly weren't stealing out of necessity. For instance, among those who appeared in court were Fitzroy Thomas, a forty-three-year-old organic chef, and Laura Johnson, a university student and the nineteen-year-old daughter of a wealthy business owner.

9. What caused England's looting and violent destruction? Some British commentators have blamed austerity measures, the lack of proper male role models, and **welfare** dependence, as well as the influence of criminal gangs and the criminal mentality on young people. Others say people rioted because it was easy to stay ahead of an underprepared police force, because others were doing it, and because they could get free stuff.

welfare: government financial assistance provided to the poor

10. But maybe the simplest explanation is the most obvious: they did it for the excitement. Bill Buford, a reporter who joined British soccer hooligans and described his experiences in his book, *Among the Thugs*, says that soccer fans engage in violent

England riot: burned police car

CCTV: Closed Circuit Television

evict: expel or remove someone from a property

the man: slang term referring to a person or organization in a position of authority (government, etc.)

cuts both ways: expression meaning that something affects both sides equally

destruction "because it is fun." Buford admits that, during his research, he got caught up in the thrill of being part of a destructive mob: "I had not expected the violence to be so pleasurable." He called the experience "intoxicating," an "anti-social kick," and an "adrenalin-induced euphoria."

11 While social media helped fuel England's disturbances—providing participants with a time and place—social media was also the undoing of many rioters. Outraged citizens created "name and shame" Facebook pages, uploading cellphone images of rioters and publically humiliating them. Police forces also used the tools of social media. They posted images from the nation's sophisticated system of **CCTV** cameras on Facebook and YouTube. With the public's help, police have identified close to two thousand looters. Many have lost their jobs, been expelled from schools, and been prosecuted by the criminal courts. The British Prime Minister has even threatened to cut people's benefits and **evict** families from social housing if their members participated in the riots.

12 Of course, text messaging and Twitter aren't to blame for the actions of a criminally-oriented minority. Social media has also helped topple dictators. The tools used by Tunisian and Egyptian revolutionaries to coordinate their 2010–2011 protests were the same tools used by apathetic Western teenagers with a taste for organized destruction.

13 Members of the technologically-savvy generation are able to thumb their noses at "**the man**" in new, exciting, but potentially dangerous ways. But nowadays, when virtually everyone carries a camera, the ability to find anonymity in a crowd may be an outdated concept. British Prime Minister David Cameron called the riots a "wake-up call" for the British. Perhaps the biggest wake-up call is for rioters who are finding out that social media **cuts both ways**.

(1072 words)

Sources: Hastings, Max. "Years of Liberal Dogma have Spawned a Generation of Amoral, Uneducated, Welfare Dependent, Brutalized Youngsters." *Mail Online*. Associated Newspapers Ltd., 10 Aug. 2011. Web.
Hui, Stephen. "UBC Student Apologizes for Role in Vancouver Riot, Criticizes Social Media Mob." *Straight.com*. Vancouver Free Press, 20 June 2011. Web.
"London Riots: More than 1000 Arrested Over Disorder." *BBC News London*. British Broadcasting Corporation, 12 Aug. 2011. Web.
Todd, Douglas. "Psychology of a Riot: They Found It Exciting." *The Vancouver Sun*. Canada.com, 17 June 2011. Web.
"The Competing Arguments Used to Explain the Riots." *BBC News Magazine*. British Broadcasting Corporation, 11 Aug. 2011. Web.

Answer additional reading and listening questions. You can also access audio and video clips online.

VOCABULARY

1 Write the letters of the best definitions in the spaces provided. The paragraph numbers are in parentheses.

Terms
1. ignited (1) _____
2. looters (2) _____
3. subsided (3) _____
4. sobbing (5) _____
5. make ends meet (5) _____
6. taken a toll (6) _____
7. thumb their noses (13) _____
8. savvy (13) _____

Definitions
a. smart; intelligent
b. caused continuing long-lasting damage
c. earn enough to pay living expenses
d. diminished
e. started
f. show derision and disdain
g. people who steal during a riot
h. crying heavily

GRAMMAR LINK AND COMPREHENSION

Combine the words in parentheses to compose each question. Some questions require that you add an auxiliary such as *do*, *does*, or *did*. Then answer each of the questions.

2. What (the difference, be) _____ between a flash mob, a flash rob, and a riot? Define the three terms.

   Flash mob: _____

   _____

   Flash rob: _____

   _____

   Riot: _____

   _____

3. When (England's riots, occur) _____?

   _____

4. What role (BlackBerries, play) _____ in England's riots?

   _____

   _____

5. In 2011, who (the rioters, be) _____ in England?

   _____

6. Why (the author, mention) _____ Fitzroy Thomas and Laura Johnson in paragraph 8?

   _____

   _____

7. (Bill Buford, participate) _____ in England's 2011 riots? See paragraph 10. ☐ Yes ☐ No

8. In 2011, why (people, riot) _____ in England? Provide at least three reasons that are mentioned in the text.

   _____

   _____

   _____

   _____

9. How (social media, cut) _____ both ways? See paragraphs 11 to 13.

   _____

   _____

   _____

10. Since 2010, (there, be) _____ any riots in your country?

    _____

SPEAKING — Flash Mob

"Invisible Dogs" flash mob in Brooklyn

In New York, the theatre company Improv Everywhere has made a series of videos about its flash mob events. The group gathers ordinary citizens and does public displays of improvisation. For example, on a cold Saturday in New York City, the world's largest train station came to a sudden halt. Over two hundred Improv Everywhere participants froze in place at the exact same second. Commuters were shocked and delighted by the site. A clip featuring this event can be found on the website of Improv Everywhere. You can also go to YouTube; simply do an Internet search using "Frozen Grand Central" or "Improv Everywhere" as keywords.

With a team of three to six students, make your own improvisation. For example, you can make your own version of a "frozen" sequence, where you and a group of students all freeze in a public space. Or you can also do another type of improvised activity in a public place. For example, you can ask some people to stare at the ceiling while sitting in the cafeteria or ask people to stand backwards in an elevator.

If you have access to a video camera, film your event and the reactions of others. In class, present what happened. Explain your process. What did you do? Also describe how people reacted.

LISTENING PRACTICE

1. Word Stress

Dictionaries use heavy black dots to show how words break into syllables. Practise identifying stressed syllables.

> **Pronunciation TIP**
>
> **HELP WITH ONLINE DICTIONARIES**
>
> Many dictionaries are available online. On *dictionary.reference.com*, the stressed syllable is indicated in bold, and by clicking on the loudspeaker, you can hear the word being pronounced. (Note that *dictionary.reference.com* also has a "Thesaurus" tab.)
>
> **co•op•er•a•tion** 🔊   [koh-op-*uh*-**rey**-sh*uh*n]
>
> From *dictionary.reference.com*

Repeat each word after the speaker. Then underline the stressed syllable. (Stressed syllables are louder and higher than other syllables.)

1	tra•di•tion•al	8	in•ven•tor•y	15	be•gin•ning
2	psy•chi•a•trist	9	lab•or•a•tor•y	16	med•i•cal
3	sec•re•tar•y	10	mo•ti•vate	17	med•i•ca•tion
4	po•ten•tial	11	mo•ti•va•tion	18	o•pe•rate
5	en•vi•ron•ment	12	hap•pen•ing	19	op•er•a•tion
6	pun•ish•ment	13	of•fered	20	de•vel•oped
7	in•vent	14	pre•ferred	21	un•der•stand

CHAPTER 7 | Social Issues | 117

2. Word Stress in Sentences

Practise your pronunciation by repeating each sentence after the speaker. Then underline the stressed words and syllables. Note that several words may be stressed in a sentence. Also remember that negative contractions are generally stressed.

1. The crime rate has fallen recently.
2. The young man was innocent.
3. A riot is caused by many factors.
4. The police arrested some suspects.
5. Why didn't you tell the truth?
6. What happened to those people?
7. I forgot to lock the door.
8. Why don't you open a window?
9. She didn't break the law.
10. We offered to help her.

Practise your spelling by doing dictations.

LISTENING

Public Shaming

Rioting after important hockey matches has occurred in cities throughout Canada. But in 2011, something different occurred. Cellphone cameras captured images of rioters. Those images went online. And then the public shaming began. Listen to a discussion about social media and public shaming.

VOCABULARY AND COMPREHENSION

1. Fill in the missing words in the spaces provided. Choose from the words below. Also, listen to the word stress in the sentences.

   | ashamed | decisions | mentality |
   | celebration | embarrassment | Wednesday |

   Nathan Kotylak: My name is Nathan. I am seventeen years old. On _____ night, I went to Vancouver to join thousands of other people that were hoping to be part of a great Stanley Cup _____. After the game, some people in the crowd started to get out of control. I made some very bad _____, ones that I now have to live up to. I went from being a spectator to becoming part of the mob _____ that swept through many members of the crowd. In a moment, I acted in a way that is an _____ to my family, my school, my community, the Vancouver Canucks, and the city of Vancouver. I am truly _____ of what I did.

2. After the hockey riots, someone posted a photo of Nathan Kotylak online. What was Nathan doing in the photo?
   a. Stealing from a clothing store
   b. Jumping on a car
   c. Holding a burning rag near a police car

3. What happened to Nathan and his family after the photo appeared online?

   _____
   _____

Scene from Vancouver hockey riot

4. Robert Gorcak and Kimli Welsh both have sites that identify rioters. Where did they post the photos?
   a. Twitter   b. Facebook   c. YouTube

5. Some people accused Kimli Welsh of being a snitch. What is a *snitch*?
   a. An informer or tattletale   b. A hero   c. A spy

6. How many people viewed Gorcak's photos? _____

7. What was Robert Gorcak's intention with his website?
   a. He wanted to publicly shame people.
   b. He wanted rioters to apologize.
   c. He simply wanted to identify the rioters.

8. What does Welsh mean when she says that blaming alcohol and the mob mentality is a *cop-out*?
   a. It is a legitimate excuse.
   b. It is an insincere excuse meant to avoid punishment.
   c. It is an excuse to attack police.

9. Stan Whitman gives an example of a shame penalty imposed by the government. What is his example?
   _____
   _____

10. Is Stan Whitman comfortable with public shaming?   ☐ Yes   ☐ No

11. Describe the difference between public shaming and government shaming.
    Government shaming: _____
    _____
    Public shaming: _____
    _____

12. What is Alexandra Samuel's opinion about public shaming?
    _____
    _____
    _____

SPEAKING

Crime and Punishment

Imagine that citizens in your city rioted after a sports game. They destroyed cars and buildings in your city's downtown core.

You are the judges. Working with a team, determine the charges and suitable punishments for these rioters. You can be creative in your sentencing.

Possible charges:

arson	looting	shoplifting
break and enter	manslaughter	theft
disturbing the peace	murder	vandalism

CHAPTER 7 | Social Issues | 119

Camilla Cage

Camilla Cage is a twenty-four-year-old engineering student at a local university. During the night of the riots, she danced on the roof of a damaged car. A cellphone video also showed her laughing as she left Marla's Fashions with her arms full of stolen clothing. The boutique owner did not have enough insurance to cover the damage and went bankrupt. Camilla Cage says that she was simply having fun and following the crowd. "Everyone was doing it," she argues.

The charges: _____

The sentence: _____

Wayne Morris

This nineteen-year-old waiter was considered one of the instigators of the riot. On the night of the riot, he threw the first brick through a store window. Others soon joined him. Morris stole computers and iPads from an Apple store. Police caught him trying to sell the stolen goods on Craigslist. He says that he was stoned on the night of the riot and does not remember what happened. He has one previous arrest for shoplifting.

The charges: _____

The sentence: _____

Eric Brown

This twenty-six-year-old is a pro golfer. He was drunk on the night of the riots. He set a garbage can on fire and threw the can through a store window. The fire spread to a nearby apartment block, and the tenants had to be evacuated. One elderly tenant succumbed to smoke inhalation and died. Brown says that the crowds influenced him. He expresses sincere regret for his actions.

The charges: _____

The sentence: _____

Your Conclusion

Which rioter deserves the most severe punishment? _____

Explain why. _____

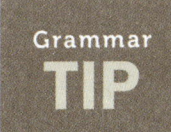

Grammar TIP

Modals

Use the base form of verbs after modals.

              base form
   He **should pay** for the damages.

To learn more about modals, see Unit 7 in *Avenues 2: English Grammar*.

READING STRATEGY

Appreciating Short Stories

Unlike essays, short stories are works of fiction that have little or no relation to true events.

When you read a short story, ask yourself the following questions.

Plot: What happens? What is the moment of greatest tension in the story?

Setting: When and where does the story take place? How does the location add to the mood or atmosphere of the story?

Character: What are the main characters like? Are they believable? How do the characters help the story move forward?

Theme: What does the author want to tell us? What is the underlying meaning?

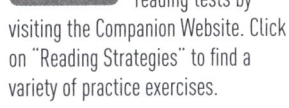 Prepare for your reading tests by visiting the Companion Website. Click on "Reading Strategies" to find a variety of practice exercises.

Born in 1862, William Sydney had problems with the law. Committed to a federal penitentiary for four years, he began writing under the pen name O. Henry. He eventually wrote hundreds of stories and was wildly successful, but in the end, O. Henry squandered his money and died impoverished. Read one of his most successful stories.

The Cop and the Anthem

BY O. HENRY

PART 1

1. On his bench in Madison Square, Soapy moved uneasily. Wild geese honked overhead, and a dead leaf fell in Soapy's lap. That was Jack Frost's card, letting all know that winter was **near at hand**. Soapy realized that the time had come for him to prepare for the coming cold.

near at hand: coming soon

2. The winter ambitions of Soapy were not of the highest. Three months on the Island was what his soul craved. He would love three months of assured room and board and congenial company, safe from the cops.

3. For years, the hospitable Blackwell Island Penitentiary had been his winter quarters. Just as his more fortunate fellow New Yorkers had bought their tickets to Palm Beach and the Riviera each winter, so Soapy had made his annual sojourn to the Island. And now the time had come. On the previous night, three newspapers, distributed

CHAPTER 7 | Social Issues | 121

ward off: keep away

beneath his coat and over his lap, had failed to **ward off** the cold as he slept on his bench. So the Island was on Soapy's mind.

scorned: felt contempt for

4 He **scorned** the provisions made in the name of charity for the city's dependents. In Soapy's opinion, the law was more benign than philanthropy. There were institutions, municipal and humanitarian, where he could receive lodging and food. But to someone with Soapy's proud spirit, the gifts of charity come with a price. Perhaps he wouldn't pay in coins, but he would pay in humiliation of the spirit for every benefit he received at the hands of philanthropy. Every bed of charity included a personal inquisition. It is better to be a guest of the law, which does not **meddle unduly** with a gentleman's private affairs.

meddle unduly: interfere unnecessarily

5 Soapy decided to go to the Island, and set about accomplishing his desire. There were many easy ways of doing this. The most pleasant was to dine luxuriously at some expensive restaurant, and then, after declaring insolvency, be handed over without a **fuss** to a policeman. An accommodating judge would do the rest.

fuss: commotion

6 Soapy left his bench and strolled out of the square and across the pavement. On Broadway he halted at a glittering cafe. Soapy had confidence in himself. He was clean-shaven, his coat was decent, and his neat black tie, given to him by a lady missionary, was around his neck. Only his pants were a problem. If he could reach a table in the restaurant without arising suspicion, success would be his. The part of his body that showed above the table would raise no doubt in the waiter's mind.

7 Sauntering casually to a table, Soapy thought about roasted mallard duck with a bottle of Chablis, and then Camembert, ending with a demitasse of coffee. The total would not be so high that the management would want severe revenge, but it would leave him filled and happy for the journey to his winter refuge on Blackwell Island.

Blackwell Island Penitentiary

8 As soon as Soapy set foot inside the restaurant door, the head waiter's eyes fell upon his frayed trousers and decadent shoes. A pair of strong hands turned him around and silently guided him to the sidewalk.

9 It seemed that Soapy's route to the coveted island was not to be an epicurean one. He would have to think of another solution. At a corner of Sixth Avenue, he spotted a store's lit-up window, with its beautifully displayed **wares**. Soapy took a large stone and heaved it through the glass. People came running around the corner, a policeman in the lead. Soapy stood still, with his hands in his pockets, and smiled at the man in the blue uniform.

wares: products

10 "Where's the man who did that?" inquired the officer excitedly.

11 "I might have had something to do with it," said Soapy, in a friendly tone.

12 The policeman's mind refused to accept Soapy's confession. Men who smash windows do not remain at the scene to chat with the local cop. They **take to their heels**. The policeman saw a man halfway down the block running to catch a car. With his club in his hand, the officer rushed off to pursue the stranger. Soapy, feeling disgust in his heart, strolled off, annoyed that he was unsuccessful yet again.

take to their heels: run away

PART 2

13 On the opposite side of the street was a simple, unpretentious restaurant. It catered to large appetites and small wallets. This place would accept Soapy's worn-out shoes and telltale trousers without challenge. At a table, he sat and

consumed beefsteak, pancakes, doughnuts, and pie. And then to the waiter, he admitted that he did not have even the smallest coin in his pockets. "Now, get busy and call a cop," said Soapy. "And don't keep a gentleman waiting."

14 "No cop for you," said the waiter, with a voice like butter. "Hey, give me a hand," the waiter yelled to his fellow server. Then the two waiters pitched Soapy outside, onto the sidewalk. Soapy lay there with his left ear smashed against the ground. Slowly, he arose, joint by joint, and beat the dust from his clothes. Arrest seemed but a rosy dream. His island prison seemed very far away. A policeman who stood before a drug store two doors away looked at Soapy, laughed, and strolled away.

15 Dejected, Soapy wandered for five blocks before his courage returned, permitting him to consider another way to be caught. This time he spotted the perfect opportunity. "This will be **a cinch**," he thought. A young attractive woman was standing before a store window gazing at its display. Two metres from the window, a large policeman with a severe demeanour leaned against a fire hydrant.

a cinch: easy

16 Soapy's plan was to assume the role of the despicable skirt-chaser. The refined and elegant appearance of his victim and the proximity of the conscientious cop encouraged him to believe that he would soon feel the pleasant official clutch upon his arm that would insure his winter accommodations on the little island.

17 Soapy straightened his tie, dragged his shirt cuffs out of his sleeves, set his hat at a tilt, and sidled toward the young woman. He stared at her, coughed, stood in front of her, smirked, and presented her with some contemptible suggestions. Out of the side of his eye, Soapy saw that the policeman was watching him fixedly. The young woman moved away a few steps and again bestowed her absorbed attention upon the items in the window. Soapy boldly stepped to her side, raised his hat, and said, "Don't you want to come and play in my yard?"

18 The policeman was still looking. The persecuted young woman just had to lift her finger, and Soapy would be en route to his island haven. Already he could feel the cozy warmth of the station house. The young woman faced him and, stretching out a hand, caught Soapy's coat sleeve. "Sure, Mike," she said joyfully, "if you'll buy me a beer."

gloom: pessimism

19 Soapy was overcome with **gloom**. He seemed doomed to liberty. The young woman clung to his arm and propelled him away, past the cop. At the next corner, Soapy shook off his companion's arm and ran off. Out of breath, he stopped at a brightly lit street. Men in cosy jackets and women in fur coats moved happily in the wintry air.

20 A sudden fear seized Soapy. Some dreadful magic had made him immune to arrest! He felt a rising panic. Up ahead, there was another policeman lounging in front of a theatre. Soapy decided he would provide some "disorderly conduct." With his best acting, he yelled drunken **gibberish** at the top of his harsh voice. He danced, howled, and ranted, disturbing those around him.

gibberish: unintelligible meaningless speech

goose egg: zero score in a sports game

21 The policeman twirled his club, turned his back to Soapy, and remarked to a citizen, "It's one of those university kids celebrating the **goose egg** they gave to Hartford College. He's noisy but harmless. We have instructions to leave them be."

22 Disconsolate, Soapy stopped making a racket. Would a policeman ever lay hands on him? The island prison seemed like an unattainable utopia. He buttoned his thin coat against the chilly wind.

CHAPTER 7 | Social Issues | 123

PART 3

23 In a convenience store, Soapy saw a well-dressed man lighting a cigar. The man had put his silk umbrella beside the door. Soapy stepped inside, grabbed the umbrella, and sauntered off with it slowly. The man with the cigar quickly followed Soapy out of the store and onto the street.

24 "My umbrella," he said, sternly.

25 "Oh, is it?" sneered Soapy, adding insult to his little larceny. "Well, why don't you call a policeman? I took your umbrella! There is a policeman straight ahead!" The umbrella owner slowed his steps. The policeman looked at the two men curiously.

26 "Of course," said the umbrella man, "that is—well, you know how these mistakes occur—if it's your umbrella, I hope you'll excuse me—I picked it up this morning in a restaurant—If you recognize it as yours, why—I hope you'll accept—"

27 "Of course it's mine," said Soapy, viciously.

28 The ex-umbrella man retreated. The policeman hurried to help a tall blonde cross the street.

29 Soapy walked eastward past a construction site. He hurled the umbrella into an excavation hole. He muttered against the men who wear badges and carry clubs. Eventually, Soapy walked back toward Madison Square, for the homing instinct survives even when the home is a park bench.

30 But on an unusually quiet corner, Soapy stopped. There was a quaint old church. Through one violet stained-glass window, a soft light glowed. In the distance, Soapy heard an organist playing an anthem on a great organ. Sweet music drifted out to Soapy's ears and held him, awed. He leaned against the iron fence, listening attentively.

31 The moon was above, so beautiful and serene. Sparrows twittered sleepily in the branches of nearby trees. The anthem that the organist played transported Soapy to the days when his life contained such things as mothers and roses and ambitions and friends.

32 Soapy's receptive state of mind and the music from the old church created a sudden and wonderful change in his soul. With horror, he realized the pit into which he had fallen, filled with degraded days, unworthy desires, and dead hopes. His heart responded thrillingly to this novel mood. A strong impulse moved him to fight against his desperate state. He would **pull himself out of the mire**! He would make a man of himself again! He would conquer the evil that had taken possession of him! There was time; he was comparatively young. He would resurrect his old ambitions and pursue them with determination.

pull himself out of the mire: remove himself from poverty and homelessness

33 Those solemn but sweet organ notes had set up a revolution in him. Tomorrow, he would go downtown and find work. A fur importer had once offered him a place as driver. He would find him tomorrow and ask for the position. He would be somebody in the world. He would—

34 Soapy felt a hand laid on his arm. He looked quickly around into the broad face of a policeman. "What are you doing here?" asked the officer.

35 "Nothing," said Soapy.

loitering: hanging around an area for no reason (perhaps with the intention of committing a crime)

36 "Then come along," said the policeman. "You are under arrest for **loitering**."

37 "Three months on the Island," said the Magistrate in the Police Court the next morning.

(1848 words)

Source: Adapted from Henry, O. "The Cop and the Anthem." *New York World*. 1904. Print.

COMPREHENSION

1. Where does the story take place? _____

2. Describe Soapy. Guess his age and describe what he is wearing.
   _____
   _____
   _____

3. Where does Soapy usually sleep at night?
   _____

4. Why does Soapy want to get to Blackwell Island Penitentiary?
   _____
   _____

5. Approximately how long does Soapy want to stay in the island prison?
   a. Three days   b. Three months   c. Three years

6. Why does Soapy prefer prison over humanitarian aid? See paragraph 4.
   _____
   _____
   _____

7. In paragraph 19, the author says that Soapy seemed "doomed to liberty." What does he mean?
   _____
   _____

8. List the six ways that Soapy tries to get arrested. Briefly write what happens.
   - _____
   - _____
   - _____
   - _____
   - _____
   - _____

9. What is the twist at the end of the story? What unexpected thing happens?
   _____
   _____
   _____

CHAPTER 7 | Social Issues | 125

Vocabulary BOOST

Act It Out

The verbs listed below appear in the short story, "The Cop and the Anthem." You will be asked to define the verbs in one of the sections below.

- Working with a partner, define the verbs in your section using context clues and a dictionary. (The paragraph numbers are indicated in parentheses.)
- Then act out your verbs for the pairs of students who worked on the other sections. Those students must guess which verbs correspond to your actions.

A

stroll (6) _____	heave (9) _____
saunter (7) _____	pitch (14) _____
spot (9) _____	beat (14) _____

B

gaze (15) _____	sidle (17) _____
clutch (16) _____	smirk (17) _____
drag (17) _____	cling (19) _____

C

twirl (21) _____	mutter (29) _____
sneer (25) _____	lean (30) _____
hurl (29) _____	twitter (31) _____

WATCHING

Ask Me Anything: I'm Homeless

CBC's *Connect* asked Robert Thomas Payne to answer questions from strangers. He sat at a table, and behind him was a sign that said, "Ask Me Anything: I'm Homeless." Watch to see what happens.

COMPREHENSION

1. Why does Robert Thomas Payne agree to answer questions?

   _____
   _____

2. In what city does Robert live? _____

3. Where does Robert usually sleep?

   _____

4. A little boy asks two questions. Basically, what does the boy want to know?

   _____
   _____

5. Someone asks, "How can I know if you'll just spend money on your substance abuse problem?" What does Robert say to the man?

   _____
   _____

6. What was Gibson's story? What was the main reason that he became homeless?

_____

_____

7. Gibson gives Robert some advice. What is the advice?

_____

8. At the end of the video, who does Robert accept help from?

_____

DISCUSSION

Why do people become homeless? Think of some causes for homelessness.

Take Action!

WRITING TOPICS

Write an essay about one of the following topics. For more information about essay structure, see Writing Workshops 2 to 4. Also, before handing in your work, refer to the Writing Checklist on the inside back cover.

1. **Flash Mobs**

   Write an essay about the benefits of flash mobs. Explain what flash mobs contribute to daily life. In your introduction, provide background information about flash mobs. Your first body paragraph can be about the benefits of flash mob for the participants, and the second paragraph about the benefits for the spectators.

   In your body paragraphs, present examples from Improv Everywhere. Search for the group's website on the Internet, and view some of their "missions." Describe what happened in some of the flash mob videos that you watched. Also, if you created your own flash mob video, describe what happened.

2. **Simple Crimes**

   In an essay, argue that ordinary people break the law in small ways. Think about some laws pertaining to driving, littering, cycling, theft, jaywalking, drugs, drinking, and so on. Present two or three laws that people break. In your body paragraphs, provide specific examples from your life or the lives of people you know. You can also quote from the readings in this chapter.

3. **The Homeless**

   O. Henry's "The Cop and the Anthem" was published in 1904. Why do people still read it? In an essay, explain how the story is still relevant today. Develop two or three supporting arguments. Think about Soapy's personality and his actions. In your body paragraphs, you can compare Soapy to the real-life homeless man, Robert Thomas Payne, from the video *Ask Me Anything: I'm Homeless*.

4. **Protests and Riots**

   Write an essay about protests and/or riots. Find a focus for your essay. In your body paragraphs, include a quotation from "Flash Mobs, Flash Robs, and Riots." Also give examples from your life or the media. You can discuss one of the following topics.

   - Explain the difference between a protest movement and a riot. For example, you can discuss the "Occupy" movement or student protests and compare them to hockey riots, England's riots, or any other riot.

■ VOCABULARY REVIEW

Identify any words that you do not understand and learn their meanings.

☐ homeless
☐ kidnap
☐ mob
☐ riot
☐ saunter
☐ shame
☐ shoplift
☐ smuggle
☐ sneer
☐ snitch
☐ thug
☐ witness

- Discuss why people participate in riots. Why do ordinarily honest people suddenly engage in activities such as looting or vandalism?

5 Social Issues

Write about a problem that is facing your college, town, city, or region. In your introduction, explain why there is a problem. Then in your body paragraph, provide either two reasons that the problem exists or two ways to solve the problem.

SPEAKING TOPICS

A Problem and a Solution

Speak about a problem in your community. Find an issue that directly affects you or someone you know. For example, you can discuss body image, drug use, dropout rates, drinking and driving, gambling, and so on. The problem can be serious (drug use, drinking and driving) or trivial (lack of parking spaces at your college).

- Introduce your topic. Begin with historical information, general information, or an anecdote. End your introduction with your thesis, or main point.
- Then prove that there is a problem. Include an anecdote about you or about someone you know, or discuss a well-known event in the news.
- Explain how to solve the problem. Suggest at least two actions that individuals, schools, governments, or others can take to improve the situation.
- Conclude your presentation. End with a quotation, suggestion, or prediction.

> **SPEAKING PRESENTATION TIPS**
>
> - **PRACTISE YOUR PRESENTATION** and time yourself. Speak for about three minutes or for a length determined by your teacher.
> - **USE CUE CARDS.** Do not read! Put about fifteen words on your cue cards.
> - **BRING VISUAL SUPPORT.** You can bring an object, picture, poster, photograph, or PowerPoint presentation, or create a short video.
> - **CLASSMATES WILL ASK YOU QUESTIONS** about your presentation. You must also ask your classmates about their presentations. Review how to form questions before your presentation day.

 To practise vocabulary from this chapter, visit the Companion Website.

Revising and Editing

REVISE FOR ADEQUATE SUPPORT
EDIT FOR MODALS

A good essay should include supporting details. (To learn more about adequate support, see Writing Workshop 3, page 149.)

Read the short essay and follow these steps.

1 In the body paragraphs, add examples from your life or from the life of someone you know. Your examples will help make the paragraphs more complete.

 Correct seven errors with verb tense shifts or modals, not including the example.

In most Canadian provinces, the legal drinking age is eighteen. Youths must ~~showing~~ **show** their government ID before they can enter a club or buy beer in a store. But the government should change that law. Our government should removing all rules about the drinking age.

First, most young people drink before they were eighteen. Almost everyone can enters clubs with a fake ID. For example, _____
_____
_____
_____

With no legal age, alcohol would not be so exciting. It would became a normal part of life. In some European countries, people drink alcohol with the family meal. For instance, _____
_____
_____
_____

In the past, the government shouldn't had made laws about a legal drinking age. The laws have cause problems. Now, many teens drink too much alcohol because they wanted to be "cool." They don't know how to handle social drinking. Maybe one day the law will change.

Grammar TIP

Tense Consistency

Do not make illogical verb tense shifts. Only shift tenses when the time frame really changes.

When I was sixteen, I went into a club and ~~drink~~ **drank** a beer.

To learn more about tense consistency, see Unit 3 in *Avenues 2: English Grammar*.

READING SUPPLEMENT

Alicia Gifford is a writer and editor. In this abridged short story, the main character deals with a very difficult moral dilemma.

Toggling the Switch

BY ALICIA GIFFORD

1. On Tuesday, Toni meets her lover, Gordon, for dinner downtown at the Water Grill. They each have a martini at the bar while they wait for a table. They get seated and both order salads. She orders salmon; he orders lobster and a bottle of Chardonnay.

2. He fidgets, distracted. She drinks her wine and wonders what his problem is. "What's up?" Toni asks.

3. He looks at her. "Elaine's pregnant," he says. Elaine is Gordon's wife.

4. Toni puts the fish in her mouth and chews slowly. With her mouth full she says, "*Really*? And you're the lucky daddy?"

5. He reddens. "We shared a bottle of champagne followed by cognac a few weeks ago, our anniversary. That's the first time we've had sex in months. She wants the baby. She wants to get counselling. She knows I've been having an affair."

6. Toni picks up the glass of Chardonnay and takes three large gulps. This is fine, she tells herself. This is a good thing. She's been insane to carry on with him anyway. If the financial firm she works for found out she's been having an affair with a client—a *married* client—she'd be fired. Still—

7. "I told her I'd try," he says, staring at his plate. "I told her I'd go to counselling, that I'd work on the marriage."

8. "You should," she says. "I never intended for this to go on this long anyway. I'm *glad* she's pregnant," she says. "Congratulations. It's fine. I was going to tell you it was over tonight anyway." Which is almost true. She's been planning to break up the last three or four times they were together; it's just that she is too fond of him.

9. The wine gives her a great buzz. She feels reckless and dramatic.

10. "I'll miss you," she says. She raises her glass in a toast. "Here's to great fun." She empties her glass and stands up and hardly staggers when she walks away, slowly, swaying her hips with deliberate sensuality.

11. *Just one of those things*, Toni sings out loud, walking out of the restaurant. It's June but the evening is cool. A few tears well in her eyes, and she enjoys the self-pity. She's exhilaratingly drunk. She calls her friend Lenny and asks if he's busy. He's a TV producer between jobs, spending his time playing video games and getting high. He also sells pot now and then.

12. She drives to his apartment in Santa Monica in her SUV 4Runner. She'd left her BMW Z3 Roadster at home tonight, and she's glad. When she gets to Lenny's, he offers her a beer and a bong hit, and she tells him about the break-up.

13. "Life 101," he says. "No affairs with married men."

toggle: snap or turn on

14 "Yeah, well." He's right, of course. She didn't know why she had to **toggle** her self-destruct switch to feel alive. She's not hungry but eats some of his cold pizza anyway and drinks a beer. They do a couple of shots of tequila. They watch *Blade Runner* on Lenny's home theatre system and pass the bong.

crash: sleep; stay

15 "I'm going to bed," Lenny says abruptly. "**Crash** on the sofa."

16 "I've got to get home," she says, rubbing her neck.

17 "You can't drive."

18 "I'm fine. I've got to work in the morning," she says, but Lenny's already nodded off in his cushy leather recliner.

19 She gets in her car and drives with the windows down. She lets the cold air smack her face. She gets off the freeway at Ventura Boulevard because she's weaving. She blasts a Pearl Jam CD as she carefully drives the empty streets heading east, coming to complete stops and minding the speed limit. She feels hopeful. She wants to meet someone and have a relationship, something healthy and decent. The breakup is an opportunity, a good thing. Decency, that's what she needs in her life.

20 The moon is out. It's nearly one in the morning when she gets to her neighbourhood. The streets are deserted, the houses dark. She heads up the narrow canyon to her house, looking forward to her bed, when ahead of her a kid shoots down a steep driveway on a skateboard, straight at her. A split second in her headlights—wide blue eyes, a blur of freckles, Spiderman pajamas—then the thick thud of impact—and he disappears.

21 She throws the car into park and gets out. He's in the gutter, head against the curb. In the streetlight she sees blood coming from his ears and mouth. His eyes are half open, dead. Dark, wet tissue—with hair—hangs off the concrete.

22 She shakes violently. She squats, checks for a pulse with her fingers on his neck—his head rolls—a ghastly angle—and blood and brain leak out. She gets her cellphone—no service in this part of the canyon. She runs up to the house that he came from and rings the bell and pounds the door, but no one's there.

23 She goes back to where he's lying and tugs his pajama top down to cover his belly. "Oh honey, I'm so sorry, so sorry," she says, her face slimy with tears and mucus. She staggers to her car, gets in, and shifts into gear. She pulls away, slowly at first, and then faster, not looking back.

24 She'll call from her house. She'll call the police and explain everything, how he came from nowhere, how she tried to report it.

25 Inside her garage, she shuts the door. She looks at the car; the boy's body has left a slight impression on the grill. She's wide awake—but drunk. She can taste and smell alcohol. She's stoned on pot. What's going to happen if she calls to report a hit and run?

sober: not drunk

26 He's dead. Nothing can help him. It wasn't her fault. A **sober** person would've hit him. She'll hold off calling until the alcohol clears her system. She sits, staring, seeing the boy, the broken egg of his head.

27 She dozes, and now it's dawn. She calls her office and leaves a message that she's sick. She turns on the TV. Around eight she hears it on the Channel 4 News. "A hit and run has claimed the life of nine-year-old Freddy Lasko in Burbank while he was apparently out skateboarding." The boy's parents were out of town

attending a funeral. The boy's sister found him around three when she came home. The phone number of the Burbank police flashes on the screen.

28 She should call a lawyer, but only tax and corporate attorneys come to mind. She needs a criminal lawyer—*Christ*. She covers her mouth with her hands. She can't make decisions right now; she needs to clear her mind, to rest. She takes a sleeping pill and turns off the phone.

29 She wakes up at four in the afternoon, disoriented. The memories start to download, and she runs to the bathroom to vomit.

30 She turns on the news. "Still no clue as to who killed Freddie Lasko early this morning while he rode his skateboard," a reporter says, standing outside the family home. "Police need your help …"

'Sup: short form of "What's up?"

31 The phone rings. "Hey, it's Lenny. **'Sup**? I called your office and they said you were sick."

32 "Oh God, Lenny. Something's happened. Something awful." Sobbing, she tells him about the accident.

33 "Call a lawyer and turn yourself in," he says.

34 "I'll lose my job. I'm up to become a partner."

35 "You killed a kid."

36 "He was skateboarding at one in the morning. His parents left him with a flaky sister. If anything, *they're* negligent."

37 "I told you not to drive."

38 "He came from nowhere, down a driveway, like a shot."

39 "Tell them you were with me. Tell them we played Scrabble, drank tea. You drove home, killed him, and panicked. They don't have to know you were drinking. Get a lawyer."

40 "Look, I'll talk to you later," she says.

41 She slips on some sweatpants, a T-shirt, and her walking shoes. She walks down to the boy's street. She gets near the house, strolling with deliberate nonchalance, a decent woman out for an afternoon walk. Police are there; the area around the curb is taped off. A media truck is parked on the street. Toni walks to where a detective stands under a tree, smoking a cigarette.

42 "I heard about this on the news," she says. "Any progress?"

43 The detective looks at her, blows smoke through his nostrils, then crushes the cigarette under his foot. He picks up the butt, puts it into a baggie, and pockets it. "You live around here?" he asks.

44 "A few blocks away."

45 "Housewife?" he asks.

46 "Uh, no." She smiles at him, but he doesn't smile back. She regrets talking to him—what was she thinking? She's the proverbial perp, returning to the scene of the crime.

47 "Not much to go by. Probably someone local," he says. "Where did you say you live?"

48 She tells him the wrong street.

49 "Humour me. Where were you between midnight and three in the morning?"

50 "Me?"

51 "Just doing my job, ma'am," he says. "Where were you last night? Do you mind?"

52 "I spent the night in Santa Monica. I was with my friend."

53 He reaches into his pocket, pulls out his card, gives it to her. "If you hear anything."

54 She takes the card, and he pulls out a notebook. "What kind of a car do you drive, anyway?" he asks.

55 "I kind of resent this," she says, mustering indignation.

56 "You got something to hide?"

57 "I drive a BMW Z3," she says.

58 "Bet you look good in it, too," he says. Now he smiles. "Anyone at your place drive an SUV?"

59 "No."

60 "Know anyone in the neighbourhood with an SUV?"

61 "Maybe 50 percent, around here," she says.

62 He laughs. "Yeah, that's about right," he says. "Why don't you give me your name and address, phone number too. That way we'll know we already talked to you."

63 She makes it all up.

64 "Have a nice day," he says. He puts the notebook away and pulls out another cigarette.

65 She starts to walk away when a woman approaches her from one of the houses. "He gave me the third degree too," she says. "I live across from the Laskos. I almost killed Freddy twice—see? Those are my skid marks right there." She points to the black tire marks in the street. "That kid loved to come streaking down that driveway. I told his parents he'd get killed. His folks were in Sacramento. Jody—that's Freddy's sister—was out on a date or something when it happened." The woman shakes her head. "How anyone could leave a dead kid like that is beyond me."

66 "Horrible," Toni croaks. She's light-headed, nauseated. She breaks into a cold sweat.

67 The woman leans in, drops her voice. "I heard the coyotes got to him. I heard his head was nearly *gone*—can you imagine? That poor doll finding her brother like that?"

68 "*God*." Toni covers her mouth. She sees the detective eyeballing them as they talk.

69 "Losing a kid's gotta be the worst," the woman says, shaking her head. She looks at her watch. "Nice talking to you." She hands Toni a business card. "Think of me for all your real estate needs."

70 Toni gets back to her house. In the garage she inspects the 4Runner again, moving her fingers over the slight dent in the polished chrome.

71 The phone rings. It's Lenny. "Have you done anything?" he asks.

72 "Uh-uh." She swallows. "It wasn't my fault. I'd be screwed if I turned myself in now. It's a conservative firm, Lenny. They don't make felony manslaughterers partners."

73 "What about your car?"

74 "Slight dent," she says. "I can bash it into a tree. I'll get rid of it."

75 "Talk to a lawyer."

thirty pieces of silver: reference to the money Judas was offered to betray Jesus

busted: caught by the police

duping: fooling; tricking

76 "I don't want to tell anyone else about this."

77 "It's wrong."

78 "Legally, yes. I feel bad for the Laskos, but would knowing who did it and ruining my life really help them?"

79 "What if they offered a reward and I turned you in? Would that be wrong in Toni World?"

80 Is he messing with her—when she's desperate for his support? She rotates the heel of her hand into her eye socket. "**Thirty pieces of silver**? You're my *friend*. I've *trusted* you with this."

81 Lenny's quiet a moment. "Yeah, I'm messing with you." Another pause. "How are you going to live with yourself? At least talk to a lawyer and see what he says."

82 "You're sure taking the moral high ground, for a *drug dealer*."

83 A long pause. "Maybe so." More silence. "Look, think about it. Think about spending your life worrying that you've been **busted** every time the phone rings or someone comes to your door. It's not worth it. My two cents." He hangs up.

84 She goes over everything once again. It wasn't her fault. Why should she ruin her life over this stupid accident? She comes up with a plan to write an anonymous note and explain there was nothing she could do. She'll put a wad of cash in it, for Jody, to get therapy, or clothes, or whatever she needs. It's Toni's fault that Jody found her brother like that, with half his head eaten away by coyotes.

85 Lenny will get over it.

86 It hits her then, the cool thrill of getting away with all this, **duping** the dour detective. A memory intrudes from junior high school. She'd been cruel to a boy—Jimmy Rodriguez—with a clubfoot and a little deformed arm. She'd made fun of him.

87 She limps in circles now, in her living room, dragging her foot and folding her arm up against her chest in the Jimmy Rodriguez Clubfoot Shuffle. She sees her reflection in the polished black granite of her fireplace, and she wonders who in the world she might be.

(2301 words)

Source: Adapted from Gifford, Alicia. "Toggling the Switch." *Narrative*. Narrativemagazine.com, n.d. Web.

COMPREHENSION: THE SETTING AND THE CHARACTERS

1. Where does the story take place?
   _____

2. What is Toni's economic or social class? Look for clues in the story.
   _____
   _____

3. In paragraph 5, Gordon said, "She knows I've been having an affair." What is an affair?
   _____

4. Who is Lenny?
   _____

COMPREHENSION: THE PLOT

5 In about five sentences, summarize what happens up to the moment of the accident. (Use the present tense in your summary.)

A woman is in a restaurant with her married lover.

_____
_____
_____
_____
_____
_____
_____
_____

6 Why does Toni decide to hide her crime? Think of at least three reasons.

_____
_____
_____
_____

7 How did the following people contribute to Freddie Lasko's death? If you think someone is completely innocent, mention it.

Freddy's parents: _____
_____
_____

Freddy's sister: _____
_____
_____

Lenny: _____
_____
_____

Toni: _____
_____
_____

COMPREHENSION: THE THEME

8 What are some messages or lessons in the story? Think of at least two messages.

_____
_____
_____
_____
_____

READING GROUP ACTIVITY

Work with a team of at least six students. Then choose a partner in your team. Each pair of students must choose one of the following activities. Work with your partner to complete your activity.

Group 1: Questions

With your partner, create ten comprehension questions about the story. To prepare, divide a sheet of paper into ten pieces. Write the questions on one side of the papers and the answers on the other side. Do not copy any of the questions from pages 134-135. (Note: Do <u>not</u> make questions about vocabulary.)

Create questions using a variety of question words. When you rejoin your teammates, show them the questions, one at a time. The other teammates must try to answer each question. Then you can turn each paper over and show the answer.

Group 2: Definitions

Working with your partner, choose ten difficult words from the story. To prepare, divide a sheet of paper into ten pieces. Write the words on one side of the papers and their definitions on the other side. Indicate which paragraph the word is in. When you rejoin your other teammates, show them the words in sequence. Using context clues, your teammates must guess what the words mean.

Group 3: Story Arc

With your partner, write ten to fifteen sentences that sum up the story in chronological order. To prepare, divide a sheet of paper into ten or more pieces. Write one sentence on each piece of paper. When you join the rest of the group, your other teammates must put the parts of the story in the correct order.

WRITING

1. Write a paragraph describing the mistakes that the characters made. Discuss Toni, Lenny, Freddy, and Freddy's sister. Explain what each person should have done or should not have done.

2. Write an essay about "Toggling the Switch." Explain who is responsible for the boy's death. In your introduction, you can provide a brief summary of the story. Then, in your first body paragraph, present the main suspects and explain how they contributed to the boy's death. In your second body paragraph, explain who is mainly responsible. In your conclusion, end with a suggestion, prediction, or quotation.

3. Write an essay about drinking and driving. You can discuss why people drink and drive, or you can present reasons why they shouldn't drink and drive. In your body paragraphs, refer to events in your life and in "Toggling the Switch."

4. Write about the benefits of reading. Explain how literature (stories and essays) entertains and informs us. Provide two or three supporting ideas. In your body paragraphs, refer to specific essays and stories that you have read in the course.

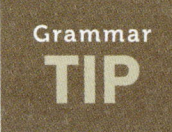

Past Forms of Modals

When you write the past forms of *should*, *could*, or *would*, remember to use *have* + the past participle.

She **should have taken** a taxi home.

To learn more about modals, see Unit 7 in *Avenues 2: English Grammar*.

WRITING WORKSHOP 1
Writing a Paragraph

Paragraph Structure

A **paragraph** is the main building block of most types of writing. Paragraphs can stand alone, or they can be part of a longer structure such as an essay, a letter, or a report. A well-written paragraph includes the following elements.

A **topic sentence** expresses the main idea.

Supporting sentences provide details and examples.

> **Our government needs to invest more in health care.** First, waiting lists for surgical procedures are unacceptably long. My uncle had to wait eighteen months for his heart surgery, and he almost died. Also, emergency rooms are understaffed. When I broke my leg playing hockey, I spent fourteen hours in a hospital waiting room. Finally, many citizens cannot find a family doctor. Thus, they do not get the medical attention that they need. Our health system needs more money and more doctors.

A **concluding sentence** brings the paragraph to a satisfying close.

Generating Ideas

When you are given a writing assignment, the first step is to choose a topic. If your teacher gives you a broad topic, you will have to narrow it down and make it more specific. There are various strategies that you can use to narrow down and develop a topic. The three most common strategies are **freewriting**, **brainstorming**, and **clustering**.

FREEWRITING

When you **freewrite**, you write without stopping for a certain period of time. You record whatever thoughts come into your mind without worrying about spelling, grammar, or punctuation.

> EXAMPLE: I have to write about tipping. I don't know what to write. Who should we tip? It's sometimes hard to know. At a fast-food counter, should I tip the cashier? Also, when the service is bad, maybe we shouldn't tip? But it could be the cook's fault. Or maybe the restaurant doesn't have enough staff. What else? Maybe tips should be put on the bill.

BRAINSTORMING

When you **brainstorm**, you create a list of ideas. If necessary, you can stop and think while you are creating your list. Once again, don't worry about grammar or spelling—the point is to generate ideas.

> EXAMPLE: Topic: Voting
> – Who votes more—men or women?
> – Compulsory voting
> – How to make people care about politics
> – Skepticism of public
> – Political scandals

CLUSTERING

When you **cluster**, you draw a word map. You might write a topic in the centre of the page and then link ideas to the central topic with lines. When you finish, you will have a visual image of your ideas.

EXAMPLE:

Compose It	Generate Ideas

Use freewriting, brainstorming, or clustering strategies to generate ideas about one of the following topics.

    Travel   The good life   Beauty ideals

Other topics: _____

The Topic Sentence

After you have generated ideas, you can plan your **topic sentence**. The **topic sentence** tells the reader what the paragraph is about. Your **topic sentence** should have the following qualities:

- It is the most general sentence in the paragraph.
- It expresses the **topic**.
- It includes one **main or controlling idea** that expresses the writer's opinion, attitude, or feeling about the topic. The controlling idea can appear at the beginning or end of the sentence.

                              topic   + controlling idea
The commercialization of traditional holidays <u>helps our economy</u>.

                controlling idea   + topic
<u>Many celebrations lose their meaning</u> **when holidays are commercialized**.

WRITING EXERCISE 1

Circle the topic and underline the controlling idea in each topic sentence.

EXAMPLE: (Insomnia) is caused by several factors.

1. Marriage is becoming an outdated institution.
2. Three strategies can help you speak with strangers.
3. Moving to a new country is a traumatic experience.
4. There should not be racial profiling at borders.
5. The public school system is underfunded.

WRITING EXERCISE 2

Write a topic sentence for each paragraph.

1. Topic sentence: _____

_____

First, art education teaches children to be creative thinkers. Early exposure to art promotes right-brain thinking. Also, art classes help children have a greater appreciation for the beauty that surrounds them daily. It helps them slow down and appreciate moments in life. Above all, making art is fun. It provides a stress-free moment in a child's day.

2. Topic sentence: _____

_____

First, it would have a big front porch. There would be a space where people can sit and watch what is happening on the street. Also, my ideal house would have windows that face the sun. During winter months, sun exposure helps people feel more positive. The kitchen would have enough room for the family to gather together during meals. Finally, my ideal house would have a lot of calm colours on the interior walls.

Topic Sentence Problems

Your topic sentence should have a topic and a controlling idea. It should not be too narrow or vague. Do not write "My topic is" or "I will write about."

Narrow: University tuition is over $5000 per year.
(The topic is too narrow. It would be difficult to write a paragraph about this.)

Vague: The financial costs are huge.
(What financial costs? The topic is unclear.)

No controlling idea: I will talk about paying for university.
(What is the main point? This says nothing relevant about the topic.)

                                controlling idea   topic
Good topic sentence: Universities should not raise tuition fees.

WRITING EXERCISE 3

Revise each topic sentence. Make it have a clear and specific focus.

EXAMPLE: This paragraph is about drunk driving.
       Topic sentence: Our country needs stronger laws about drunk driving.

1. I will write about Internet addictions.

Topic sentence: _____

_____

2. My lab partner's name is Angelica.

Topic sentence: _____
_____

3. A decision changed my life.

Topic sentence: _____
_____

4. I will discuss travel.

Topic sentence: _____
_____

Compose It — Write Topic Sentences

Write a topic sentence for each of the following topics or choose your own topics. Remember to narrow your topic to give it a specific focus. Also determine what your controlling idea is.

Travel   The good life   Beauty ideals

Your topic(s): _____

EXAMPLE: *Topic:* __Travel__   *Specific topic:* __Camping__
Topic sentence: __The best type of vacation is to go camping.__

1. Topic: _____ Specific topic: _____

   Topic sentence: _____
   _____

2. Topic: _____ Specific topic: _____

   Topic sentence: _____
   _____

3. Topic: _____ Specific topic: _____

   Topic sentence: _____
   _____

Generating Supporting Ideas

When you finish writing a topic sentence, you must think of specific evidence that supports it. You can include the following types of support: facts, examples, anecdotes, and quotations.

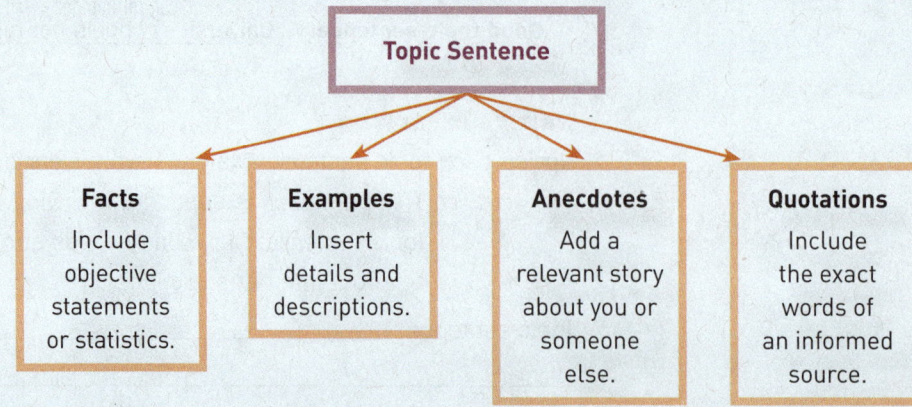

WRITING EXERCISE 4

Read the paragraph below and complete the tasks that follow.

People have many misconceptions about autism. First, a common myth is that children with autism never learn. Dr. R. Barnes, an autism specialist, says that about 60 percent of parents worry that their children will not improve. In fact, many programs can help children with autism, and every child responds differently. Another incorrect belief is that autistic children cannot speak. In reality, many can communicate quite well. My cousin Tara is autistic, and she speaks quite easily. Yet another myth is that those with autism will never show affection. Dr. Melinda Grant says, "Many people with autism learn to show their emotions." The greatest myth is that people with autism cannot have productive lives. Dr. Temple Grandin proves that is not true. Grandin, who was born in Boston and diagnosed with autism at age two, went on to get a doctorate. She has published essays and spoken widely about her experiences. Today, she is a highly regarded professor at Colorado State University. Autism covers a wide spectrum, so everyone should remember that not all individuals with autism are alike.

1. Underline the topic sentence.

2. Number the four main supporting ideas.

3. Find an example of each type of supporting detail.

   Fact: _____

   Fact (Statistic): _____

   Anecdote: _____

   Quotation: _____

4. Highlight the concluding idea.

WRITING EXERCISE 5

Generate three supporting ideas for the following topic sentences.

1. The best things in life are free.

   1. _____
   2. _____
   3. _____

2. People learn many things when they travel.

   1. _____
   2. _____
   3. _____

Compose It — Write a Stand-Alone Paragraph

Choose one topic sentence from the Compose It section on page 140. Then, on a separate sheet of paper, write a complete paragraph about the chosen topic. Include supporting facts and examples. Also, ensure that your paragraph is coherent. Every sentence should relate to the topic sentence.

WRITING WORKSHOP 2
Writing an Essay

Essay Structure

An **essay** is divided into three parts: an **introduction**, a **body**, and a **conclusion**. Look at the following example to see how different types of paragraphs form an essay.

Making the Right Choices

The **introduction** generates interest in the topic.

This winter, there was weird weather all over the planet. Winter storms hit the southern United States, and in Canada, there was unusually warm weather that caused flooding in some areas. Ice flows are melting in the Arctic. **In their daily actions, people should make the right choices for the environment.**

The **thesis statement** tells the reader what the essay is about.

Each **body paragraph** begins with a **topic sentence**.

When shopping, consumers should never use plastic bags. Everyone can use inexpensive and reusable cloth bags instead of plastic shopping bags. There are rolled-up cloth bags that fit in a pocket or purse. Also, consumers should remember to bring their cloth bags to the mall and not just to grocery stores. The bags can carry new clothing, tools, and electronic items. For example, I bring cloth bags to stores such as Walmart and Canadian Tire.

Each **body paragraph** contains details that support the thesis statement.

Citizens should use bicycle- and car-sharing programs. If someone can afford to buy a car, it doesn't mean he or she should buy one. Instead, people should consider joining a car-sharing network. Montreal, Toronto, and most major cities have them. Bike-sharing is also widely available. For example, in Montreal, people can pick up and drop off Bixi bikes in areas throughout the city.

The **conclusion** briefly restates the main points and ends with a suggestion, prediction, or quotation.

Everybody should consider the impacts that their daily activities will have on the environment. Making conscious shopping decisions is a very good way to have a big impact. As environmentalist David Suzuki says, "Our personal consumer choices have ecological, social, and spiritual consequences."

The Introductory Paragraph

The **introductory paragraph** introduces the subject of your essay. It helps your reader understand why you are writing the text. The thesis statement is the last sentence in your introduction.

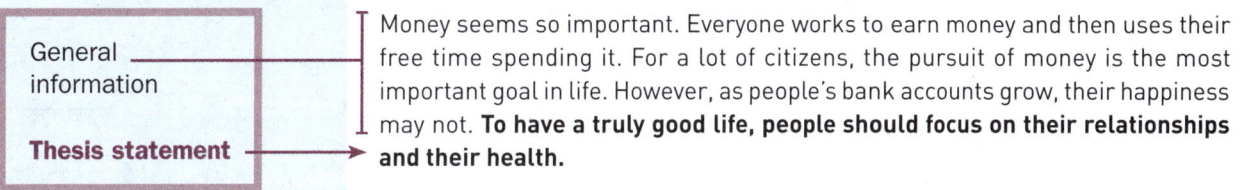

General information: Money seems so important. Everyone works to earn money and then uses their free time spending it. For a lot of citizens, the pursuit of money is the most important goal in life. However, as people's bank accounts grow, their happiness may not. **Thesis statement: To have a truly good life, people should focus on their relationships and their health.**

Writing the Thesis Statement

A good thesis statement focuses on a central idea. It presents the topic of the essay, and it includes a **controlling idea** that expresses the writer's opinion, attitude, or feeling about the topic. The controlling idea can appear at the beginning or end of the thesis statement.

topic + controlling idea
Daycares provide many advantages for small children.

controlling idea + topic
There are many problems associated with **putting children in daycare**.

CHARACTERISTICS OF AN EFFECTIVE THESIS STATEMENT

An effective thesis statement expresses an attitude or point of view. It should not be an obvious fact, a vague statement, or a question. Do not announce the topic by using expressions such as *I will write about*, *I think*, or *My essay is about*.

Announcement: I will write about sports.
(This sentence has no controlling idea.)

Obvious: Many people play sports.
(This is an obvious fact. It does not express an attitude or opinion.)

Vague: Injuries are a big problem.
(Injuries caused by what? For whom are they a problem?)

Question: Why do people love team sports?
(This question does not express a point of view or attitude about the topic.)

Effective thesis statement: Team sports, such as hockey and football, have advantages and disadvantages.

Guided Thesis Statement

Your teacher may want you to list your main arguments in your thesis statement. To do this, mention both your main point and your supporting points in one sentence.

Weak: When people travel, they can learn many things. I will explain how they learn about other languages, beliefs, and customs.

Better: When people travel, they can learn about other languages, beliefs, and customs.

It is not necessary to prolong the introduction with extra sentences that provide details about your main points.

WRITING EXERCISE 1

Examine each statement. If it is a good thesis statement, write **TS** on the line. If it is weak, identify the type of problem(s).

    A – announcement   **Q** – question   **V** – vague   **O** – obvious

EXAMPLE: This essay is about recycling.   A

1. Pollution is a big problem. _____
2. To avoid potential problems, people should never post embarrassing photos and cruel words online. _____
3. In this paper, I will discuss the causes of riots. _____
4. Canada should not build more prisons for two reasons. _____
5. Some health problems are serious. _____
6. Why should college students learn a second language? _____
7. Being a soccer coach is rewarding physically and emotionally. _____
8. In my essay, I will discuss youth crime and why it happens. _____

The Thesis Statement and Topic Sentences

What is the difference between a thesis statement and a topic sentence?
An essay has <u>one</u> thesis statement and several topic sentences. The **thesis statement** is in the introduction, and it explains what the essay is about. **Topic sentences** are in the body paragraphs. Each topic sentence explains what the body paragraph is about.

Thesis statement: Social networking sites have some positive benefits.

Topic sentence 1: People can remain in contact with friends in other cities.

Topic sentence 2: Social websites can help people plan protests and revolutions.

WRITING EXERCISE 2

Read the following thesis statements. Then generate two topic sentences that support each thesis statement.

1. Thesis statement: Many people in our culture take dangerous risks to look beautiful.

Topic sentence 1:

Topic sentence 2:

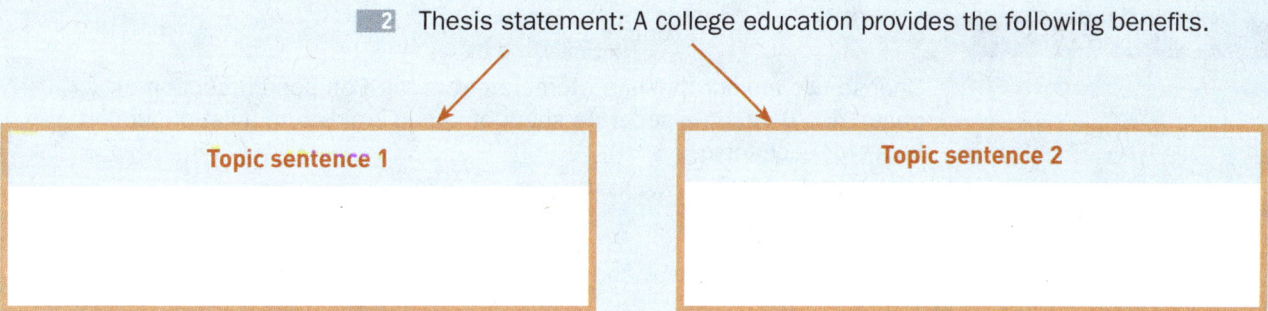

Compose It — Write Thesis Statements

Write three thesis statements. You can choose one or more of the following topics, or you can choose your own topics. Remember to narrow each topic to give it a specific focus.

Music   Technology   Addictions

Your topic(s): _____

EXAMPLE: Topic: __Music__   Specific topic: __Classical music__
Thesis statement: __Classical music is the best type of music.__

1. Topic: _____   Specific topic: _____
Thesis statement: _____
_____

2. Topic: _____   Specific topic: _____
Thesis statement: _____
_____

3. Topic: _____   Specific topic: _____
Thesis statement: _____
_____

The Supporting Ideas

In an essay, each body paragraph provides supporting evidence for the thesis statement.

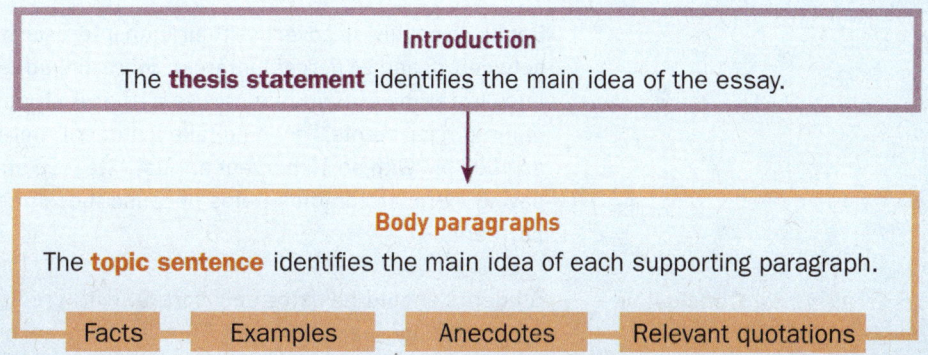

Compose It — List Supporting Ideas

Choose two of your thesis statements from the Compose It section on page 145. Then, on a separate sheet of paper, brainstorm a list of supporting ideas for each topic.

WRITING EXERCISE 3

Read the following essay and then complete the tasks below.

1. At the beginning of each body paragraph, write a topic sentence. The topic sentence should sum up the main points of the paragraph in an interesting way.

2. After reading the entire essay, create an effective thesis statement. The thesis statement expresses the main point of the essay.

Rethinking Credit Cards

Introduction

When students enter college, they receive credit card advertisements from banks. The ads explain why it is a great idea to get a credit card. For sure, the advantages are numerous. It is easy to book a flight online or buy an item from eBay.

Thesis statement: _____
_____
_____

Body paragraph 1

Topic sentence: _____
_____
_____

People think, "I'll buy it now and pay for it later." My friend Nathaniel fell into that trap. He planned to use his card "only for emergencies," but within six months he built up a $3000 debt. He went over his limit and had to pay a penalty. Then, to his surprise, he received an offer to raise his credit limit to $5000. Clearly, credit card companies encourage people to overspend.

Body paragraph 2

Topic sentence: _____
_____
_____

Banks do not like to advertise their high interest rates. Bank credit cards charge between 18 and 24 percent interest. Store-linked cards charge up to 35 percent. Lucy Lazarony of *Bankrate.com* says that if students stick to just making the minimum payments, "it would take a student more than twelve years to pay off a $1000 bill with an 18 percent annual rate." So students like Nathaniel end up paying extra for common items because they don't really consider the interest payments.

Conclusion

Students should be extremely careful with credit cards if they really want to avoid getting deeply in debt. They should learn to budget and also inform themselves about how interest rates work. Al Nagy, a financial planner, warns, "Credit is a double-edged sword: a good thing if used wisely but harmful if one gets carried away."

Creating an Essay Plan

A plan (or outline) is a visual map that shows the essay's main and supporting ideas. It also includes details for each supporting idea.

Thesis statement: Parents spoil their children for many reasons.

1. **Topic sentence:** People are not educated about good parenting skills.

   Supporting idea: Schools do not teach how to be a good parent.
   Detail: My high school and college don't offer parenting courses.
   Supporting idea: Some people may follow the example of their own parents.
   Detail: Add quotation from psychologist Manuel Reyes.

2. **Topic sentence:** Some parents are motivated by guilt to overspend on their children.

   Supporting idea: They spend very little time with their children.
   Detail: Add statistic about the disappearance of the family dinner.
   Supporting idea: They buy gifts, unnecessary clothing, etc.
   Detail: Add anecdote about Dan M., who never sees his kids and spoils them.

Concluding suggestion: Colleges should have adult education courses in parenting.

WRITING EXERCISE 4

Read the following thesis statement. Then create an essay plan. Generate two supporting ideas and write topic sentences. Then provide details for each supporting idea.

Thesis statement: When young people move away from home, they quickly learn the following lessons.

Topic sentence 1: _____
_____

Details: _____
_____
_____

Topic sentence 2: _____
_____

Details: _____
_____
_____

Topic sentence 3: _____
_____

Details: _____
_____
_____

Compose It — Create an Essay Plan

Develop an essay plan for a topic that your teacher suggested, or choose ideas that you have developed in this workshop.

Introduction
Thesis statement: _____
_____

Body paragraph 1
Topic sentence: _____
_____

Supporting idea: _____
_____

  Details: _____
  _____
  _____

Supporting idea: _____
_____

  Details: _____
  _____
  _____

Body paragraph 2
Topic sentence: _____
_____

Supporting idea: _____
_____

  Details: _____
  _____
  _____

Supporting idea: _____
_____

  Details: _____
  _____
  _____

Conclusion
(Think of a final suggestion, prediction, or quotation.) _____
_____
_____

WRITING WORKSHOP 3

Improving Your Essay

Write an Effective Introduction

Write your **introduction** after you have planned the main points of your essay. A strong introduction will capture the reader's attention and make him or her want to read the rest of your essay.

Introduction Styles

You can begin the introduction with an attention-grabbing opening sentence, such as a question or a surprising statement. Then you can develop your introduction in several ways. Experiment with any of the following introduction strategies:

- Give **general background information**.
- Provide **historical background information**.
- Tell an **interesting anecdote**.
- **Define** a concept.
- Present a **contrasting position** or idea that is the opposite of the one you will develop.

> **TIP**
>
> **Thesis Statement Placement**
>
> Most introductions begin with sentences that introduce the topic and lead the reader to the main point of the essay. The thesis statement is generally the **last sentence** in the introduction.

WRITING EXERCISE 1

Read the following introductions. Underline each thesis statement and then identify the introduction style that was used.

1. Last summer, my friend Celine worked at a children's camp. One day, her boss took her aside. He explained that some parents had complained about Celine's Facebook page, which had photos of her smoking marijuana. Celine was shocked and embarrassed. People should never post certain types of photographs online.

   What is the introduction style?

   ☐ Anecdote ☐ General ☐ Historical ☐ Definition

2. Back in the early days of humanity, people fought tribal wars using clubs, bows, and arrows. When gunpowder was invented, they killed each other with cannons and rifles. Then, during the twentieth century, nations developed bombs, including nuclear weapons, that could destroy entire cities. These days, many countries own weapons of mass destruction. War is clearly a part of human history. There are three major reasons that countries go to war.

   What is the introduction style?

   ☐ Anecdote ☐ General ☐ Historical ☐ Contrasting position

3. In restaurants, it is common to see diners sending text messages instead of talking with their companions. In coffee shops, people take up tables for hours as they work on their laptops. And on buses, people have loud conversations on their cellphones. In this digital age, parents should teach their children about social etiquette.

What is the introduction style?

☐ Anecdote ☐ General ☐ Definition ☐ Contrasting position

4. What is oversharing? It is putting really personal photos on Facebook or another site. It is sending private thoughts to many people on Twitter. It is letting people in cyberspace know deep intimate secrets. It is even just telling friends and coworkers about really sensitive information. Oversharing has some negative consequences for people.

What is the introduction style?

☐ Anecdote ☐ Historical ☐ Definition ☐ Contrasting position

5. The Internet is fantastic. People can play games online and spend hours feeding their animals with Farmville. They can share photos with friends on a social networking site. Sites like YouTube have great videos that everybody can watch. However, cyberlife is not always as good as it seems. The Internet is addictive and can have very bad effects on people's lives.

What is the introduction style?

☐ Anecdote ☐ General ☐ Historical ☐ Contrasting position

WRITING EXERCISE 2

Choose one of the following thesis statements or write your own thesis statement. Then, on a separate piece of paper, write three different introductions. Choose a different style (anecdote, general, historical, or definition) for each introduction.

1. Living in this country has advantages and disadvantages.
2. Music helps people relax and release their emotions.
3. There are several reasons that people become addicted to Facebook.

Your topic: _____

Remember the following:
- End each introduction with your thesis statement.
- Label each introduction with the style that you are using.

Write an Effective Conclusion

Your concluding paragraph should do three things.
- It should restate the thesis.
- It should summarize your main points.
- It should make an interesting closing statement. You can end with a suggestion, a prediction, or a quotation. (You can go to a quotations website such as *quotationspage.com* to find a good closing quotation.)

For example, here is a conclusion for an essay about war.

Remind the reader of your main points.

End with a prediction or suggestion.

> In conclusion, people fight wars for three major reasons. Sometimes national leaders want more territory and the money that comes with it. Other times, religious or racial intolerance causes wars. Finally, the most common reason is revenge. People should remember the words of Mahatma Gandhi: "An eye for an eye leads to a world of the blind."

Avoiding Conclusion Problems

To make an effective conclusion, avoid the following pitfalls:
- Do not contradict your main point or introduce new or irrelevant information.
- Do not apologize or back down from your main points.
- Do not end with a rhetorical question. (A rhetorical question is a question that won't be answered; for example, "When will people stop worrying about their appearance?")

WRITING EXERCISE 3

Underline the topic sentence in each body paragraph. Then write an introduction and a conclusion.

Introduction: _____
_____
_____
_____
_____
_____
_____
_____

Body paragraph 1: First, people judge the appearance and actions of celebrities. If a celebrity such as Lady Gaga gains weight or looks too thin, it becomes front-page news. If a celebrity makes a mistake or has a mental health problem, everyone judges him or her. Sometimes, the stress leads to meltdowns, like that of Britney Spears. Professor Charles Figley of Florida State University says that celebrites are "very vulnerable to the personal evaluations of other people. The public is ultimately in control of whether the celebrity's career continues."

Body paragraph 2: Furthermore, celebrities cannot have normal family lives. Many celebrities have stalkers, and they require bodyguards to protect their families. Aidan Quinn, an actor, said that women slip notes to him even when he is having dinner with his wife. And the children of celebrities also suffer. The paparazzi follow Angelina Jolie's children and take photos of them. A few years ago, some magazines insulted her daughter Shiloh just because she dressed like a boy. So the families of celebrities suffer.

…

Conclusion:
_____
_____
_____
_____
_____
_____
_____

Revise for Coherence

Your writing should have coherence. In other words, it should be easy to understand. Connections between ideas should be logical. You can use different words and expressions to help the reader follow the logic of a text.

- **Coordinators** connect ideas inside sentences. Common coordinators are *and*, *but*, *or*, *yet*, and *so*.

    The video game is violent, **but** most people don't care.

- **Subordinators** join a secondary idea to a main idea inside a sentence. Some common subordinators are *although*, *after*, *because*, *before*, *if*, *unless*, and *until*.

    Even though I probably won't win, I often buy lottery tickets.

- **Transitional words** or phrases connect sentences and paragraphs. Common transitional words are *first*, *however*, *therefore*, *of course*, and *in conclusion*. Generally put a comma after transitional words and expressions.

    First, both singers write about political issues.

WRITING EXERCISE 4

The words and expressions below illustrate different functions. Write a definition or translation beside any words that you do not understand.

Chronology	first*	_____	next	_____
	second*	_____	suddenly	_____
	third*	_____	then	_____
	after that	_____	finally	_____
	meanwhile	_____	eventually	_____
Addition	additionally	_____	moreover	_____
	in addition	_____	as well	_____
	furthermore	_____	also	_____
Example	for example	_____	for instance	_____
	in fact	_____	to illustrate	_____
Emphasis	above all	_____	surely	_____
	clearly	_____	of course	_____
	in fact	_____	undoubtedly	_____

Contrast	although	_____	however	_____
	even though	_____	nevertheless	_____
	on the other hand	_____	on the contrary	_____
Concluding idea	to conclude	_____	therefore	_____
	in short	_____	thus	_____
	to sum up		in conclusion	_____

*Do not write *firstly*, *secondly*, or *thirdly*, etc. It is preferable to write *first*, *second*, and *third*, etc.

WRITING EXERCISE 5

Add appropriate subordinators or transitional expressions in the spaces provided. Do not use the same expression more than once.

Eating meat is terrible for the health. [1](chronology) _____, eating meat can shorten a person's lifespan. [2](example) _____, the animal fat in red meat contributes to heart disease and colon cancer. [3](contrast) _____ a hamburger tastes great, it can damage a person's arteries.

[4](addition) _____, meat might contain hormones and antibiotics. Growth hormones are banned in Canada. [5](contrast) _____, Canadian suppliers sometimes include growth additives.

[6](chronology) _____, eating meat is bad for the environment. [7](emphasis) _____, raising cattle contributes to global warming. [8](example) _____, farmers in Brazil destroy rain forests to create pastures for their farm animals. [9](addition) _____, eating meat contributes to world poverty. In many countries, more grain is given to farm animals than to people.

[10](conclusion) _____, if people want to have good health and help the planet, they should stop eating meat.

Identify Common Essay Problems

Before you hand in an essay, make sure that you revise and edit your work. Look for errors in structure and correct any grammar and punctuation mistakes that you notice. Try to avoid the following common essay problems.

Problem: Unclear Thesis and Topic Sentences

Ensure that your thesis statement has a topic and a point of view. Your topic sentences should support your thesis statement.

WRITING EXERCISE 6

What are the problems with the following thesis statements? Write better thesis statements on the lines provided.

1. It is time to decide which country is better: Canada or the United States.

   Problem: _____

   Revised thesis statement: _____
   _____

2. In this essay, I am going to talk about video game addictions.

   Problem: _____

   Revised thesis statement: _____
   _____

WRITING EXERCISE 7

Read the following thesis statement. Notice that the two topic sentences do not support the thesis. Explain what is wrong with the topic sentences, and then correct them.

Thesis statement: There are two ways to have a very good life.

Topic sentence 1: People always have too much stress.

   Problem: _____
   _____

   Revised topic sentence 1: _____
   _____

Topic sentence 2: Money doesn't make people feel happy.

   Problem: _____
   _____

   Revised topic sentence 2: _____
   _____

Problem: Insufficient Supporting Details

In an essay, each body paragraph must include supporting details. Often, you find statistics, quotations, or facts from secondary sources. If you don't do any research, it is still possible to make your examples relevant.

ESSAY WITHOUT RESEARCH

You are not required to do research in this course. However, you can still have a well-developed essay. In your body paragraphs, provide specific examples from one or more of the following sources:

- Your life
- The lives of people you know
- Events in history
- Events in the media
- The lives of well-known people
- Information from readings or videos in this course

Weak: Insufficient details

Second, the Internet can have bad effects on people's lives. There is an obesity epidemic because almost everyone spends too much time in front of computer screens. Also, the Internet isolates people. They would rather spend time online than be with their friends and family. Definitely, some people prefer a cyber life to a real life. So the Internet can have a bad impact on people's lives.

When the paragraph is expanded with specific examples, it becomes more convincing. Ideally, try to include examples from readings or videos that you have studied in this course.

Better: With specific examples

Second, the Internet can have bad effects on people's lives. There is an obesity epidemic because almost everyone spends too much time in front of computer screens. Also, the Internet isolates people. They would rather spend time online than be with their friends and family. **For example, in the text, "My Personal History of E-Addiction," Steve Almond says that his one-year-old child "gets frantic" when he goes on the computer. He realizes that his computer addiction deprives his children of attention.** Definitely, some people prefer a cyber life to a real life. **When my brother lost his job, instead of looking for another job, he passed all his time chatting on the computer and looking for a girlfriend.** So the Internet can have a bad impact on people's lives.

WRITING EXERCISE 8

Add supporting details to the following body paragraphs of an essay.

Thesis statement: Team sports have advantages and disadvantages.

Body paragraph 1: First, sports have physical and emotional benefits. Many team sports involve a lot of physical exertion. For example, when I was a child, _____ _____ _____ .

Also, team sports help people bond and create solid friendships. For instance, _____ _____ _____

Body paragraph 2: However, there are also disadvantages with some sports. Certain sports involve violent hitting, and athletes can develop serious head injuries or spinal injuries. _____ _____ _____ .

Also, some athletes travel at such high speeds that they risk their lives. _____ _____ _____ .

Problem: Body Paragraphs Lack Unity

Each body paragraph should focus on one main idea that supports the thesis statement. Here are two common errors to check for when you revise your body paragraphs.

- **Rambling paragraphs:** The paragraphs in the essay ramble on. Each paragraph has several topics and lacks a clearly identifiable topic sentence.
- **Artificial breaks:** A long paragraph is split into smaller paragraphs arbitrarily, and each smaller paragraph lacks a central focus.

WRITING EXERCISE 9

When a piece of writing is not broken into logical paragraphs, it is difficult to read. The selection below would be easier to read if it were broken into separate paragraphs.

Complete the following tasks:

1. Read the selection and add a paragraph break where it is appropriate.
2. Underline two topic sentences.

Many pedestrians regularly break the law. When people arrive at a crossing with traffic lights, they are supposed to wait for the walk signal, yet jaywalking is common. Raul Guzman, a science student, says that he crosses between intersections and ignores red lights. Kate Shapiro, a hairdresser, also admits that she always crosses when the "Don't Walk" signal is blinking if there is no traffic. "It is ridiculous to wait when I know I can cross safely," she argues. Pedestrians are not the only ones who break laws. Cyclists also disrespect traffic laws. For example, many municipalities have bicycle helmet laws, but citizens regularly disobey the law. In some cities, bicycles must be equipped with reflectors, but many cyclists do not bother getting them. Also, cyclists regularly go past stop signs or zoom through red lights. Like many people, I often ride my bike through red lights, and I ride on sidewalks.

WRITING WORKSHOP 4

Writing an Argument Essay

In argument writing, you take a position on an issue and then defend it. In other words, you try to convince somebody that your point of view is the best one.

Taking a Position

The thesis statement of an argument essay should express a clear point of view. It should be a debatable statement. It should not be a fact or a statement of opinion.

Fact: Many companies have labour unions.
(This is a fact and therefore cannot be debated.)

Opinion: I think that Walmart should be unionized.
(This is a statement of opinion. Nobody can deny that you feel this way. Therefore, you should not use phrases such as *In my opinion*, *I think*, or *I believe* in your thesis statement.)

Argument: Walmart should be unionized.
(This is a debatable statement.)

WRITING EXERCISE 1

Evaluate the following statements. In the blanks provided, write "F" if the statement is a fact, "O" if it is an opinion, or "A" if it is a debatable argument.

1. Some people spend too much money. _____
2. I think that Apple makes good computers. _____
3. People should change their Internet habits. _____
4. Our town needs better public transportation. _____
5. In my opinion, our town's train service is inadequate. _____
6. Some students drive to college. _____
7. I believe that subways should be free. _____
8. Subways and trains should be free for the public. _____

WRITING EXERCISE 2

Write an argument thesis statement for each of the following topics.

1. Drinking and driving
_____
_____

2. Littering and education
_____
_____

Developing Strong Supporting Ideas

In argument essays, you can use the following types of evidence as support:

- **Tell a true story.** Find stories from the news or from readings or videos that you covered during this course. You can also include personal anecdotes to support your point of view.
- **Quote respected sources.** An expert's opinion can give added weight to your argument. If you want to argue that people should not buy energy drinks, then you might quote a respected health organization.
- **Show long-term consequences.** Every solution to a problem can carry long-term consequences. For example, "People lose money when they gamble online. In the long term, online gambling can cause bankruptcies and destroy families."
- **Acknowledge opposing viewpoints.** Provide responses to opposing arguments. For example, "Divorce is painful for children, but it can make them stronger."

Using "I" in Argument Essays

In argument essays, you should not use the first-person pronoun "I" in your thesis statement or topic sentences. However, it is perfectly acceptable to use "I" in an anecdotal introduction. It is also acceptable to use personal stories when you provide supporting details.

WRITING EXERCISE 3

Read the following student essay. Underline the thesis statement and the topic sentences. Highlight any examples using the pronoun "I."

Introduction: In the past, I did not like myself. I thought my legs were too big, and I did not like my nose. I was very critical about my appearance. Over time, I realized that I had to get over my insecurities and enjoy my life. People should stop criticizing themselves and appreciate their good qualities.

Body paragraph 1: First, good health is more important than good looks. Many people just want to be beautiful, and they take risks to look better. They get plastic surgery, they develop eating disorders, and they burn themselves in tanning beds. In "Botched Tan," Sarah Stanfield wanted her skin to be darker, and she received a severe sunburn. It hurt so much that she said, "Tears brimmed up in my eyes." Also, in the past, I sometimes skipped meals and exercised too much because I didn't want to be fat. People should never damage their health just to look better.

Body paragraph 2: Furthermore, everyone has some qualities that they should appreciate. All skin colours are beautiful, and a smile can make anyone look attractive. In "Botched Tan," Stanfield realizes that she should appreciate her skin after the nurse compliments her. In my case, I may not like my legs, but people tell me that my eyes are really nice. Also, most people appreciate a good personality more than good looks. My favourite people make me laugh, and I don't care what they look like.

Conclusion: Over time, Sarah Stanfield has learned to appreciate her skin colour, and I have learned to like my body. Instead of worrying about their imagined faults, people should remember that they have good sides. They should enjoy their lives.

Melanie Roy

APPENDIX 1
Oral Presentations

Here are some points to remember when you make an oral presentation.

Planning Your Presentation

- **Structure your presentation.** Make your introduction appealing. Use facts or examples to support your main points. Make sure you include a conclusion.
- **Practise.** Your teacher will not be impressed if you pause frequently to think of something to say, or if you are constantly searching through your notes.
- **Do not memorize your presentation.** Simply rattling off a memorized text will make you sound unnatural. It is better to speak to the audience and refer to your notes occasionally.
- **Time yourself.** Ensure that your oral presentation respects the specified time limit.
- **Use cue cards.** Only write down keywords and phrases on your cards. If you copy out your entire presentation on cue cards, you could end up getting confused and losing your place. Look at the example provided.

Presentation Text

An awesome moment in my life occurred last summer when I was alone on a beach. It was dark, and my friends were camping nearby. I was on my back staring up at the sky and suddenly, I felt so small and unimportant. But at the same time, I felt very free.

Cue Card
- last summer
- alone
- beach
- friends camping
- stars
- free

Giving Your Presentation

- Look at your entire audience, not just the teacher.
- Do not read. However, you can use cue cards to prompt yourself during the presentation.
- When the assignment requires it, bring in visual or audio supports. These can help make your presentation more interesting.
- Review question forms before your oral presentation. You may have to ask questions to other students.

APPENDIX 2

Idioms and Expressions

An idiom has a different meaning than the individual words literally suggest. Review the idioms and expressions and their meanings.

Chapter 1   On the Road

a hush fell over the room	the room became quiet
eye opener	an experience that is surprising and unexpected
hail a cab	signal that you need a taxi
hit the road	start the trip; begin a journey
kick off the road trip	start the journey (by car, bus, bicycle, etc.)
feel homesick	miss your family and your home
roughing it	living simply without the comforts and conveniences of home
shoot someone a dirty look	look at someone with contempt
travel lightly	travel with very little luggage

Chapter 2   The Pleasure Principle

awesome	fantastic; magnificent
cutting-edge idea	up-to-date idea
do a botched job	do a bad job
idea has been bouncing around	idea has been spreading
there is heat around the idea	the idea is popular
perky	energetic; happy

Chapter 3   The Artistic Life

boils down to	can be summed up as
crack the circuit	become known and accepted
freak out	get excited or scared
from the get-go	from the beginning
it's a stretch	it is not believable
take matters into your own hands	take control of a situation

Chapter 4   Great Ideas

a new breed of game	a new type of game
cause a stir	create excitement
be hooked	be addicted
be a sucker	be naive and gullible
crass	crude; unrefined
create buzz	bring attention and excitement to something
go ballistic	get extremely upset
hook up with someone	meet someone
on a whim	spontaneously
on the tube	on television
teenage flame	teenage girlfriend or boyfriend

Chapter 5   The Digital Age

cash in	make money from
fruitless conversation	useless; unproductive discussion
full-blown junkie	complete addict
get frantic	get agitated
kick a habit	stop doing something
not what it's cracked up to be	not as great as people say it is
rise above the pack	get to a higher level than others in the group
the odds	the chances
thumbnail description	short descriptive summary

Chapter 6   Urban and Suburban Life

all the rage	very popular
creepy	weird; disturbing
eyesore	ugly; horrible to look at
have your eyes wide open	be realistic
have your wits about you	think clearly and be alert
glare of publicity	oppressive media attention
litterbug	someone who throws garbage in the street
method to the madness	logic to the apparent chaos
paved with great expectations	full of hopes that all will be wonderful
pixie dust had begun to fade	realistic expectations had set in
porches hugged the sidewalks	porches were close to the sidewalks

Chapter 7   Social Issues

anti-social kick	excitement from being hostile toward others
give me a hand	help me
looters	people who steal from stores during riots
marauding hordes	groups that steal and destroy
mob mentality	tendency of a group to act together
pull oneself out of the mire	take action to change and get out of a difficult situation
smirk	smile in an offensive, conceited, or smug way
take a toll	cause continuing long-lasting damage
take to their heels	run away
yell drunken gibberish	speak loudly and incoherently when intoxicated

APPENDIX 3
Description Vocabulary

The following terms describe a person's appearance and character. Use your dictionary or discuss unfamiliar terms with your teacher. You can also practise hair and clothing vocabulary on the Companion Website.

Appearance

Face	Hair		Clothing/Other	
dimples	afro	**hair colour:**	belt	**patterns:**
freckles	bald	black	dress	dots
mole	curly	blond	glasses	paisley
scar	frizzy	brunette	jacket	plaid
wrinkles	straight	grey	pants	stripes
	wavy	red	scarf	
eye colour:			shirt	**material:**
blue		**facial hair:**	shorts	acrylic
brown		beard	skirt	cotton
green		goatee	socks	leather
hazel		moustache	sweater	spandex
		whiskers	tie	suede
			underwear	wool

Character Traits

athletic	fearless	gentle	nasty	sensible	strange
boring	foolish	honest	outgoing	sensitive	talented
brave	friendly	impatient	reliable	serious	timid
careless	fun	kind	rude	shy	unique
cheap	generous	mean	selfish	smart	witty

In the Character Traits list, put an X next to any negative traits.

APPENDIX 4

Pronunciation

Pronunciation Rules

Review the pronunciation rules. Practice exercises appear in the indicated chapters. You can also visit the Companion Website to practise your pronunciation.

Present Tense: Third-Person Singular Verbs (Chapter 1)

Rules	Sounds	Examples		
Most third-person singular verbs end in an –s or a –z sound.	s z	eats goes	hits learns	says works
Add –es to verbs ending in –s, –ch, –sh, –x, or –z. Pronounce the final –es as a separate syllable.	iz	fixes places	reaches relaxes	touches watches

Silent Letters (Chapter 2)

Rules	Silent Letters	Examples		
Gn: In most words, when g is followed by n, the g is silent.	g	benign design	foreign resign	sign Exception: signature
Mb: When m is followed by b, the b is silent.	b	climb comb	dumb plumber	thumb
Kn: When k is followed by n, the k is silent.	k	knee knew	knife knit	knot know
L: Do not pronounce the l in some common words.	l	calm could	should talk	walk would
P: Do not pronounce the p in most words that begin with ps or pn.	p	pneumonia pseudonym	psychedelic psychiatrist	psycho psychotic
T: Do not pronounce the t in some common words.	t	castle Christmas	fasten listen	often whistle
W: Do not pronounce the w in some common words.	w	who	write	wrong
Gh: In some words, the gh is silent. (Note that in some words such as laugh and cough, gh sounds like f. In other words such as ghost, the gh sounds like g.)	gh	bought daughter	light though	thought weigh

Past Tense: Regular Verbs (Chapter 3)

Rules	Sounds	Examples		
When the verb ends in –s, –k, –f, –x, –ch, and –sh, the final –ed is pronounced as t.	t	asked hoped	kissed touched	watched wished
When the verb ends in –t or –d, the final –ed is pronounced as a separate syllable.	id	added counted	folded related	waited wanted
In all other regular verbs, the final –ed is pronounced as d.	d	aged cured	killed lived	moved played

Past Tense: Irregular Verbs (Chapter 3)

Rule	Sound	Examples		
When the verb ends in –*ought* or –*aught*, pronounce the final letters as *ot*.	ot	bought brought	caught fought	taught thought

Th (Chapter 5)

Rule	Sound	Examples		
To pronounce a "voiced" *th*, push your tongue between your teeth and blow gently. Voice the sound.	th (voiced)	breathe that the	them there these	this those thus
To pronounce a "voiceless" *th* sound, push the tongue between the teeth and blow gently.	th (voiceless)	breath death moth	north south strength	think three throw

H (Chapter 5)

Rule	Sound	Examples		
Pronounce the initial *h* in most words that begin with *h*.	h	hair hand handsome hangover happy	heal height help her/his hero	history home homeless hospital hurt
In some common words, the first *h* is silent.	–	heir heirloom	herb honest	honour hour

Pronunciation Help with Online Dictionaries

Many dictionaries are available online. On *dictionary.reference.com*, the stressed syllable is indicated in bold; by clicking on the loudspeaker, you can hear the word being pronounced. (Note that *dictionary.reference.com* also has a "Thesaurus" tab.)

de•vel•op [de-**vel**-*uh*p]

From *dictionary.reference.com*

APPENDIX 5

Spelling, Grammar, and Vocabulary Logs

Spelling and grammar logs can help you stop repeating the same errors. When you do new writing assignments, you can consult the lists and hopefully break some ingrained bad habits. A vocabulary log provides you with a source of new words that you can include in your writing. Keep your logs in a folder or binder and consult them when you work on your essays.

Spelling Log

Every time you misspell a word, record both the mistake and the correction in your spelling log. Then, before you hand in a writing assignment, consult the list of misspelled words. The goal is to stop repeating the same spelling errors.

EXAMPLE:

Incorrect	Correct
realy	really
exagerated	exaggerated

Grammar Log

Each time a writing assignment is returned to you, identify one or two repeated errors and add them to your grammar log. Then consult the grammar log before you hand in writing assignments in order to avoid making the same errors. For each type of grammar error, you could do the following:

1) Identify the assignment and write down the type of error.

2) In your own words, write a rule about the error.

3) Include an example from your writing assignment.

EXAMPLE: Writing Test 1   Run-On

Do not connect two complete sentences with a comma.

Bad drivers cause ~~accidents, other~~ accidents. Other drivers do not expect sudden lane changes.

Vocabulary Log

When you learn a new word, write the word and its meaning in your vocabulary log.

EXAMPLE:

Vocabulary	Meaning	Example
smug	self-satisfied	The poker winner felt smug because he often wins.

Index

A
Act Happy 32
Act It Out 30, 126
adequate support 128
adjectives 29, 64, 79, 109
Allure of Apple (The) 65
Architecture Matters 95
argument essay 157–158
Art and Plagiarism: Does Originality Matter? 52
arts quiz 40
arts survey 55
author's purpose 51

B
base form of the verb 92
body language 8
Botched Tan (The) 24
brainstorming 137

C
capitalization 18
Chaos in the Streets 104
clustering 138
cognates 3
coherence 152–153
comparatives and superlatives 102
conclusion 108, 150–151
conditionals 86
context clues 3
contractions (identify) 103
Cop and the Anthem (The) 121
crime scenes 111
Cultural Minefields 9

D
description (appearance, character) 161
dictionary 24, 117, 163

E
emotions 31
essay plan 147
essay structure 142–156
ever 83

F
fact or opinion 51
Flash Mobs, Flash Robs, and Riots 113, 117
Freewriting 137
fun, funny 34

G
generating Ideas 137
gestures (body language) 8
Gone with the Windows 86

I
"I" in essays 158
ideal house 94
idioms and expressions 55, 83, 160
inferences 75
international crossword 2
introduction 57, 143, 149–150

J
Jay Baruchel (Interview) 46

L
Listening (interview) 7, 23, 42, 68, 85, 103, 118
Listening Practice 6, 22, 41, 68, 84, 103, 112, 117
Logs (Spelling, Grammar, Vocabulary) 164

M
main idea 60
Melissa Auf der Maur (Interview) 43
modals 121
mood, moody 34
My Personal History of E-Addiction 75

N
Novelty Items 61
numbers (identify) 68

O
oral presentations 159

P
paragraph structure 137–141
plural forms 38
police reports 112
possessive forms 70, 72
present perfect 74
present tense(s) 5, 8, 20
pronounce sentences 6
Pronunciation
 – *gh* 23, 162
 – *h*, *t*, and *th* 84, 163
 – past tense verbs 41, 162, 163
 – *s* on verbs 6
 – silent letters 22, 162
 – word stress 117, 118

Q
question forms 42, 72
question practice (speaking) 27, 69

R
Reading Strategies
 – appreciating short stories 121
 – identifying main ideas 60
 – making inferences 75
 – recognizing cognates 3
 – scanning, highlighting, annotating 99
 – thinking critically 51
 – using a dictionary 24
 – using context clues 3
 – writing a summary 61
Revising and Editing
 – adequate support 128
 – comparatives and word choice 108
 – conclusion 108
 – introduction 57
 – main idea 20
 – mixed errors 91
 – modals 128
 – nouns and determiners 38
 – present tense and word choice 20
 – pronouns and question forms 72
 – sentence variety 71
 – supporting details 38
 – transitional words and phrases 91
 – verb tense and prepositions 57
Record-Breaking Travel Adventure 14

S
scanning 99
shifting point of view 54
silent letters 22
Speaking
 – Addictive Behaviour 78
 – Arts Survey 55
 – Body Language 8
 – Crime 111, 119
 – Flash Mob 117
 – Great Decisions 69
 – Greatest Country 35
 – Have You Ever …? 83
 – Living Environment 102
 – Name Game 49
 – Name That Product 65
 – Pleasure (interview) 22, 27
 – Public Service Announcement
 – Strong Emotions
 – Tech Life 74
 – Travel Interview 17
 – Trends 60
summary 61
supporting ideas 140, 145, 154–156, 158

T
tense consistency 129
thesis statement 143–145, 153, 157
topic sentence 138–140, 144, 153
travel terms 12

U
Utopian Town of Celebration (The) 99

V
Vocabulary Boost
 – Act It Out 30, 126
 – Crime-Related Vocabulary 113
 – Descriptive Adjectives 64
 – Exteriors (house) 95
 – Humour (*fun, funny*, etc.) 34
 – Idioms and Expressions 55, 83
 – Lifestyles (*suburb*, *town*, etc.) 101
 – Tech Game 89
 – Travel Terms 12

W
was or *were* 58
Watching
 – Ask Me Anything: I'm Homeless 126
 – Damn Heels 63
 – End of Suburbia 98
 – Interview with Mark Zuckerberg 79
 – Living in Denmark 35
 – Ocean Survival 12
 – TV, Afghanistan Style
Why I Travel 4
Winter Love 28
word stress 117, 118

Y
YouTube Hits 80

Photo Credits

Alamy
p. 9: © Slick Shoots. pp. 46, 47 © AF Archive. p. 50 © Jonathan Hayward. p. 99 © Ian Dagnall.

Alex and Luke: p. 7.

Allstar Picture Library: p. 79.

Bigstock
p. 13 © Otvalo. pp. 60, 69.

BMCL: p. 66.

Canadian Broadcasting Corporation: p. 64 top.

Citylights: p. 85.

Colormekatie: p. 117.

CP Images
p. 43 © Robert Wagenhoffer. p. 44 © Pendzich/Rex / Rex Features. p. 80 © BDG / Rex Features.

Gaetz, Lynne: pp. 39, 58, original painting by Lynne Gaetz.

Hugues, Graham: pp. 14, 15.

iStockphoto
p. 8 bottom centre: © Btrenkel. p. 11 top right: © Zone Creative; top left: © S. Able; bottom right: © J. Wojcik. p. 114 © Johnny Greig. p. 115 © ValMansfield. p. 119 top: © Chris Fisher. p. 123 © Pamela Moore. p. 131 © Magnilion. p. 132 © Adam Kazmierski.

Photothèque ERPI: p. 62 middle, p. 122.

Rock, Claudia: p. 105 bottom.

Shutterstock
pp. 1, 20: © Joyfull. p. 2 top: © M. Schwettmann; bottom: © D. Michail. p. 4 © Olly. p. 8 top left: © Y. Arcurs; top centre: © K. I. Harisovich; top right: © Michaeljung; middle left: © Fotocrisis; middle centre: © J. Gil; middle right: © Andresr; bottom left: © E. Titov; bottom right: © Prodakszyn. p. 10 top: © Lusoimages; middle: © Scusi0-9; bottom: © Tandaleah. p. 11 bottom left: © withGod. p. 12 © Inc. p. 17: © K. A. Valerich. pp. 21, 38 © Yellowj. p. 22 © Ximagination. p. 23 © V. Titov & M. Sidelnikova. p. 25 © Efired. p. 26 © R. Sumners. p. 27 © D. Shironosov. p. 28 © A. Kalina. p. 29 © P. Stanislav. p. 31 top left: © Iofoto; top right: © Creatista; top middle left: © J. Stitt; top middle right: © Y. Arcurs; bottom middle left: © Dudanim; bottom middle right: © S. Coburn; bottom left: © Oliveromg; bottom right: © M. Jacques. p. 32 © J. Steidl. p. 35 © L. Schoeman. p. 40 top: © S. Chawalit; bottom: © Myotis. p. 49 © James Steidl. p. 52 © kaczor58. p. 55 © Rido. pp. 59, 72 © Subbotina Anna. p. 62 © top: Scott Rothstein; bottom: © Veex. p. 64 bottom right: © Marie C. Field; bottom centre: © VIPDesignUSA; bottom right: © Utekhina Anna. p. 65 © Anneka. pp. 73, 91 © Olly. p. 74 © Tata. p. 75 © Kevin Renes. p. 76 © Feng Yu. p. 77 © Solid. p. 78 © Andresr. p. 81 © Helga Esteb. p. 83 © James Thew. p. 84 © Wallenrock. p. 87 © Sergej Shakimullin. pp. 93, 108 © Robert HM Voors. p. 94 top left: © Photobank.ch; top right: © Jorge Salcedo; bottom left: © Christy Nicholas; bottom right: © Marilyn Barbone. p. 95 top: © Karin Hildebrand Lau; bottom: © Palabra. p. 96 top: © 4745052183; bottom: © Chris Howey. p. 98 © Iofoto. p. 103 © Delicatephoto. p. 105 top left: © Thomas Skopal; top left middle: © DDCoral; top middle: © Marijus Auruskevicius; top right middle: © Rusty Dodson; top right: © Valentyna7. p. 106 © Anton Gvozdikov. pp. 110, 128 © Photocrotical. p. 112 © Corepics. p. 113 © John Kershne. p. 119 bottom, 121 © Kuzma. p. 124 top: © Katiriska; bottom: © Nils Z. p. 126 © Kuzma. p. 130 © Elnur.